THE IMPORTANCE OF

The Beatles

These and other titles are included in The Importance
Of biography series:

Alexander the Great	Adolf Hitler
Muhammad Ali	Harry Houdini
Louis Armstrong	Thomas Jefferson
James Baldwin	Mother Jones
Clara Barton	Chief Joseph
The Beatles	Joe Louis
Napoleon Bonaparte	Malcolm X
Julius Caesar	Thurgood Marshall
Rachel Carson	Margaret Mead
Charlie Chaplin	Golda Meir
Charlemagne	Michelangelo
Cesar Chavez	Wolfgang Amadeus Mozart
Winston Churchill	John Muir
Cleopatra	Sir Isaac Newton
Christopher Columbus	Richard M. Nixon
Hernando Cortes	Georgia O'Keeffe
Marie Curie	Louis Pasteur
Charles Dickens	Pablo Picasso
Emily Dickinson	Elvis Presley
Amelia Earhart	Jackie Robinson
Thomas Edison	Norman Rockwell
Albert Einstein	Eleanor Roosevelt
Duke Ellington	Anwar Sadat
Dian Fossey	Margaret Sanger
Benjamin Franklin	Oskar Schindler
Galileo Galilei	John Steinbeck
Emma Goldman	Tecumseh
Jane Goodall	Jim Thorpe
Martha Graham	Mark Twain
Lorraine Hansberry	Queen Victoria
Stephen Hawking	Pancho Villa
Jim Henson	H. G. Wells

THE IMPORTANCE OF

The Beatles

by
Adam Woog

Lucent Books, P.O. Box 289011, San Diego, CA 92198-9011

For Kathleen Wilson,
cool person,
gifted teacher,
diehard Beatles fan

Library of Congress Cataloging-in-Publication Data

Woog, Adam, 1953–
    The Beatles / by Adam Woog.
       p.   cm. — (The Importance of)
    Includes bibliographical references and index.
    Summary: Examines the cultural significance, influence,
and legacy of the English pop group.
    ISBN 1-56006-088-3 (alk. paper)
    1. Beatles—Juvenile literature. 2. Rock musicians—
England—Biography—Juvenile literature. [1. Beatles. 2. Musicians. 3. Rock music.] I. Title. II. Series.
ML3930.B39W66   1998
782.42166'092'2—dc21   97–7470
[B]   CIP
                                                         AC MN

Contents

Foreword

THE IMPORTANCE OF biography series deals with individuals who have made a unique contribution to history. The editors of the series have deliberately chosen to cast a wide net and include people from all fields of endeavor. Individuals from politics, music, art, literature, philosophy, science, sports, and religion are all represented. In addition, the editors did not restrict the series to individuals whose accomplishments have helped change the course of history. Of necessity, this criterion would have eliminated many whose contribution was great, though limited. Charles Darwin, for example, was responsible for radically altering the scientific view of the natural history of the world. His achievements continue to impact the study of science today. Others, such as Chief Joseph of the Nez Percé, played a pivotal role in the history of their own people. While Joseph's influence does not extend much beyond the Nez Percé, his nonviolent resistance to white expansion and his continuing role in protecting his tribe and his homeland remain an inspiration to all.

These biographies are more than factual chronicles. Each volume attempts to emphasize an individual's contributions both in his or her own time and for posterity. For example, the voyages of Christopher Columbus opened the way to European colonization of the New World. Unquestionably, his encounter with the New World brought monumental changes to both Europe and the Americas in his day. Today, however, the broader impact of Columbus's voyages is being critically scrutinized. *Christopher Columbus,* as well as every biography in The Importance Of series, includes and evaluates the most recent scholarship available on each subject.

Each author includes a wide variety of primary and secondary source quotations to document and substantiate his or her work. All quotes are footnoted to show readers exactly how and where biographers derive their information, as well as provide stepping stones to further research. These quotations enliven the text by giving readers eyewitness views of the life and times of each individual covered in The Importance Of series.

Finally, each volume is enhanced by photographs, bibliographies, chronologies, and comprehensive indexes. For both the casual reader and the student engaged in research, The Importance Of biographies will be a fascinating adventure into the lives of people who have helped shape humanity's past and present, and who will continue to shape its future.

IMPORTANT DATES IN THE LIVES OF THE BEATLES

1957

Paul McCartney joins John Lennon's first band, the Quarrymen, in Liverpool, England.

1958

George Harrison joins the Quarrymen.

1960

The band (guitarists John Lennon, Paul McCartney, and George Harrison, plus bassist Stu Sutcliffe) rename themselves the Silver Beatles. They tour Scotland and appear with temporary drummers in clubs in Hamburg, Germany.

1961

Sutcliffe quits the band and McCartney replaces him on bass. Brian Epstein hears the Beatles at the Cavern Club in Liverpool and becomes their manager.

1962

Drummer Ringo Starr replaces Pete Best to become the fourth permanent member of the band. Producer George Martin signs them to the Parlophone label. The Beatles' first single, "Please Please Me," is released late in the year.

1963

British Beatlemania breaks out: The first single goes to #1. The first LP also goes to #1 and stays there until replaced by the band's second LP. The band ends the year with a command performance before British royalty.

1964

The band's appearances on the *Ed Sullivan Show*, seen by the largest audience in TV history, launch American Beatlemania. Their first film, *A Hard Day's Night*, is released. The band makes its first world tour to record-setting crowds.

1965

A second movie, *Help!*, is released. The Beatles are awarded high honors, MBEs, by Queen Elizabeth. The band makes another lengthy tour of America; the fifty-six thousand at New York's Shea Stadium sets the record for the biggest concert crowd to date in history. A landmark album, *Rubber Soul*, is released.

1966

Controversy follows the Beatles: An accidental insult during their long world tour leads to death threats in the Philippines. The gruesome "butcher" album cover and John Lennon's "more popular than Jesus" statement cause an uproar in America. The *Revolver* album is released. In August the band plays its last full concert, at Candlestick Park in San Francisco, before retiring from touring.

1967

The landmark album *Sgt. Pepper's Lonely Hearts Club Band* is released during the Summer of Love. Brian Epstein dies of a drug overdose. The band forms a new organization, Apple, to oversee their business. They study with an Indian guru, Maharishi Mahesh Yogi, and release the short film *Magical Mystery Tour*.

1968

The Beatles travel to India on an ill-fated visit to their guru. "Hey Jude" becomes the biggest Beatles single to date. A full-length animated film, *Yellow Submarine*, and *The Beatles* (better known as the *White Album*) are released. Growing tensions within the band become severe.

1969

Businessman Allen Klein and attorney Lee Eastman vie to become the Beatles' manager, creating a rift between Paul McCartney and the others. John and his new love, Yoko Ono, record together and become highly visible political activists and artists. *Abbey Road*, the band's final recording together, is released. A hoax launches a "Paul is dead" rumor.

1970

After a long seclusion, Paul McCartney publicly announces that he is leaving the Beatles and releasing a solo LP. Ringo's first solo album, the *Let It Be* album (recorded before *Abbey Road*), and the documentary film *Let It Be* are also released. Paul sues the others to dissolve the partnership.

1980

John Lennon is assassinated in New York City on December 8.

1995

Two songs with vocals by John Lennon and backing added by the surviving Beatles are released as part of *The Beatles Anthology*, a massive documentary CD and video production.

Meet the Beatles

The guitar's all very well, John, but you'll never make a living out of it.

—John Lennon's Aunt Mimi

There has never been a band quite like the Beatles. There may never be one again.

The Beatles are first of all remembered for their contributions as songwriters and recording artists: From the time they burst on the music scene like firecrackers in 1963 to their breakup in 1970, the band completely dominated the world music scene. They racked up more record-breaking hits than any group in musical history. They set new standards for song composition and transformed the art of

The Beatles—(from left to right) Paul, George, Ringo, and John—in 1964, a year after they had become international sensations. The Beatles were especially innovative in performing their original songs.

Imagine a World Without the Beatles

Nicholas Schaffner, in this excerpt from The Beatles Forever, *comments on the band's lasting impact.*

"Imagine what our world might be like today, were it not for the Beatles. Rock 'n' roll as a critically acclaimed and relatively sophisticated popular art form, with words that say something and music that draws from an almost limitless variety of sources; long hair and expressive clothing on men; marijuana and 'Eastern mysticism'—all this and more might well still be practically unheard of in the mainstream of society were it not thanks (or no thanks!) to the Beatles. . . .

The Beatles were admitted into our consciousness in the guise of a low-brow fad; like the Trojan horse, there proved to be a lot more there than initially met the eye (and ear). Once snared by the cherubic looks and the tasty bubblegum, an unsuspecting world was swept off on a magical mystery tour out of which many emerged quite different people from those they might otherwise have been."

record production. They were the first successful singer-songwriters; before them, only a few popular singers performed songs they had written themselves.

But they were also the most remarkable cultural and sociological phenomenon of their time. They transformed the look, sound, and style of a generation. They won the hearts of millions with their charm and wit, and they angered many more through their controversial actions and outrageous statements. Like them or loathe them, they were the essence of their era: swinging London, the hippie movement, Eastern religion, peace and love. A phenomenon like Beatlemania, with its hysterical crowds and near-religious devotion, has appeared at other times and has often been imitated—but the intensity of Beatlemania has never been matched.

Above all, they were a unit: John, Paul, George, and Ringo—the Fab Four. They had a little help from their friends—in particular Brian Epstein, who molded their initial public image and brought them world acclaim, and George Martin, the gifted record producer who helped them perfect their sound in the studio. But the distinct personalities of John Lennon, Paul McCartney, George Harrison, and Ringo Starr produced a unique blend; without that chemistry there would have been no Beatles. As John Lennon once explained:

Still Fresh

Rock critic John Rockwell, writing in the New York Times *in 1982, reflects on the band's nearly universal appeal. The article is reprinted in* The Lennon Companion.

"If any one person or group defined that whole spectrum of dreams, accomplishments, failures and creative confusion we call the Sixties, it was The Beatles. An entire generation grew up singing these songs, and mating to them. Quite apart from their intrinsic musical value, which is considerable, an astonishing number of Beatles songs retain their power to transform roomfuls of early-middle-aged people into weepy nostalgists. Given the fact that this baby-boom generation counts as the most numerous among us, there are plenty of weepy nostalgists out there to whom The Beatles still mean a great, great deal.

[They pioneered] production styles that have yet to be surpassed, and that sound absolutely contemporary today. As much as anything else, this lasting contemporaneity defines the greatness of the band. For all their epitomisation of their time, they seem to have tapped some secret of universality. Even such songs as 'All You Need Is Love' or 'Come Together,' which might seem impossibly dated, still ring fresh. They achieved this universality by their innate talent and by the fact that their evolution, still denounced by some as a betrayal of rock, really amounted to an abandonment of rock's parochialism in favour of a broader, more lasting popular sensibility."

None of us would've made it alone, because Paul wasn't quite strong enough, I didn't have enough girl appeal, George was too quiet, and Ringo was the drummer. But we thought that everyone would be able to dig at least one of us, and that's how it turned out.[1]

Despite this reputation as adored idols who became spokesmen for their generation and shapers of fashion and thought, the Beatles remained human beings, complete with faults and failures. Some critics feel that the band merely imitated styles set by less famous sources. Many people feel that the Beatles' experiments with drug-influenced music were misguided. Their personal lives were often chaotic, and their breakup was as messy and vicious as a divorce.

In the end, they were simply four friends who formed a little band because they liked to play music. When that band suddenly became famous, these friends—growing quickly from teenagers to maturity in the world spotlight—had to deal with both the pleasures and the pains of stardom.

In many ways Liverpool, the Beatles' birthplace, was an unlikely breeding ground. Today it is world famous as their birthplace, but most Britons in the 1950s and early '60s looked down on the scruffy port city as a dirty, blue-collar backwater. Nonetheless, the Liverpool of those days nourished the band. Because it was isolated from cultural centers, it gave them the freedom to innovate and experiment. Because it was a working-class town, it fostered their down-to-earth personalities, anything-for-attention attitudes, and sarcastic wits. On top of this was the city's unusual connection with a strange new music called rock 'n' roll. This was a sound the rest of England barely knew—but one that the four young friends heard loud and clear.

1 Beginnings

The first thing we did was to proclaim our Liverpoolness to the world, and say "It's all right to come from Liverpool and talk like this."

—John Lennon

John

John Lennon was born on October 9, 1940. His father, Alfred, was a ship's waiter who abandoned his wife, Julia, before their son was born. Julia remarried a man who didn't want children, so John was raised by Julia's sister Mimi and her dairyman husband, George, in the Liverpool suburb of Woolton. Uncle George died while John was in elementary school, leaving strong-willed Aunt Mimi to raise the boy. Even after John's mother remarried, she never took John back, though he stayed with her on and off through high school.

John was a rebellious boy—"cheeky" was the Liverpool word—who early on demonstrated the wit and creativity that would make him "the smart Beatle." He loved to create stories and cartoons, and was the leader of a gang of wild boys. He was a poor student and always in trouble at school. When he was thirteen a teacher noted on his report card, "Hopeless. Rather a clown in class. He is just wasting other pupils' time."[2]

At Quarry Bank High School, John acquired a taste for flamboyant clothes and slicked-back hair. Young toughs like him were known in England as Teddy Boys, be-

A young John Lennon with his Aunt Mimi, who reared him after John's mother remarried a man who didn't want children.

John Lennon (fourth row, second from right) and classmates from Quarry Bank High School for Boys pose for a class picture in 1957. A rebellious troublemaker, John's life gained focus and purpose when he took up the guitar.

cause the clothes they wore resembled the fashions of the Edwardian era early in the century. As a young man, John used aggressiveness to get others to do what he wanted. He later recalled, "I wanted to be the leader. It seemed more attractive than just being one of the toffees [soft upper-class kids]. I wanted everybody to do what I told them to do, to laugh at my jokes and let me be the boss."[3]

In high school he discovered music was a great way to command attention. Mimi tried to interest him in conventional instruments, but he wanted something he could master right away. "I would have sent him to music lessons, the piano or violin, when he was very young. But he didn't want that," Mimi later said. "He wanted to do everything immediately, not take time learning."[4]

The answer was the guitar. Like thousands of young Britons in the '50s, John took it up in the wake of a craze for skiffle, a mix of folk music and Dixieland-style jazz. Skiffle was perfect for John; it was simple to learn and the instruments were cheap—an acoustic guitar or two, a washboard rubbed with thimbles, and a crude bass made from a mop handle, rope, and a tea cupboard. (The player plucked the rope, holding it tense between one end of the mop handle and the cupboard; the cupboard also acted as a resonator to amplify the sound.)

Aunt Mimi bought John his first guitar, and he immediately formed a band, the Quarrymen. It consisted of himself, his friend Pete Shotton on washboard, and a changing array of others. The group practiced in the bathroom at Julia's house, because they liked the echo and because she tolerated them more than the other parents.

Paul

In another part of Liverpool, Paul McCartney was developing similar interests. Born on June 18, 1942, Paul was the son of Mary, a midwife, and Jim, a dance bandleader turned cotton salesman. His parents were hard workers, but times were tough; Paul and his brother, Mike, grew up in a close-knit but financially precarious household.

When Paul was thirteen, his beloved mother died of breast cancer. The family was devastated. Jim McCartney raised the boys as best he could alone, but he was gone all day. Paul, who—like John—was bright but aggressive, indifferent in his studies, and prone to trouble, frequently got away with skipping school and dressing like a Teddy.

Much of Paul's sadness was channeled into music when, soon after Mary died, his father gave him a guitar. The boy had difficulty learning it until he discovered that although otherwise right-handed, he was a left-handed guitar player. Once Paul turned the instrument upside down and reversed the strings, the guitar barely left his hands; he even practiced while sitting on the toilet.

Paul's early taste in music differed from John's. For one thing, skiffle music bored Paul. For another, he loved the old-fashioned jazz and pop that his father had once played and that he still heard often at home. This sweet, sentimental music, which John hated, was an influence that would resurface in Paul's compositions years later.

There was one crucial similarity between Paul and John: They both loved American rock 'n' roll. The sexiness of Elvis Presley, the passion of Little Richard, the cleverness of Chuck Berry, and the sweet harmonies of the Everly Brothers spoke straight to their hearts. As Paul later recalled, "Every time I felt low I just put on an Elvis [record] and I'd feel great, beautiful. I'd no idea how records were made and it was just magic. 'All Shook Up'! Oh, it was beautiful!"[5]

John Lennon was also a fan. Early in 1956, he heard "Heartbreak Hotel," Elvis Presley's first number-one hit in America. That was all he needed. His Aunt Mimi recalled:

> From then on, I never got a minute's peace. It was Elvis Presley, Elvis Presley, Elvis Presley. In the end I said, "Elvis Presley's all very well, John, but I don't want him for breakfast, dinner and tea."[6]

Just Give Me That Rock 'n' Roll Music

John and Paul were lucky; Liverpool was the best possible place in England to hear new American music. For most of the country, the pop music scene was dull and bland. The British Broadcasting Corporation (BBC) was England's sole radio and TV source, and the tightly controlled, government-run network considered rock 'n' roll vulgar and dangerous. As a result, most Britons found Elvis Presley, who was beginning to tear up the American music scene, a distant and faintly bizarre phenomenon; to them, pop meant either skiffle or insipid singers like the squeaky-clean teen idol Cliff Richard.

"We Were Hicksville"

John Lennon recalls Liverpool in this quote from Jann Wenner's book-length interview Lennon Remembers.

"We were the ones that were looked down upon as animals by the Southerners, the Londoners. The Northerners in the States think that people are pigs down South and the people in New York think West Coast is hick. So we were hicksville.

We were a great amount of Irish descent and blacks and Chinamen, all sorts there. It was like San Francisco, you know. That San Francisco is something else! Why do you think Haight-Ashbury and all that happened there? It didn't happen in Los Angeles, it happened in San Francisco, where people are going. LA you pass through and get a hamburger.

There was nothing big in Liverpool; it wasn't American. It was going poor, a very poor city, and tough. But people have a sense of humor because they are in so much pain, so they are always cracking jokes. They are very witty, and it's an Irish place. It is where the Irish came when they ran out of potatoes, and it's where black people were left or worked as slaves or whatever.

It is cosmopolitan, and it's where the sailors would come home with the blues records from America on the ships. There is the biggest country and western following in England in Liverpool, besides London—always besides London, because there is more of it there.

I heard country and western music in Liverpool before I heard rock and roll. The people there—the Irish in Ireland are the same—they take their country and western music very seriously. There's a big heavy following of it. There were established folk, blues and country and western clubs in Liverpool before rock and roll and we were like the new kids coming out."

But things were different in Liverpool. As the closest English port to North America, it was full of young sailors who regularly visited the United States. Many were music fans who brought back the latest records by rock 'n' roll and rhythm-and-blues (R&B) artists. This influx of American music was augmented by U.S. soldiers still stationed at Burtonwood, a nearby air force base that had been the largest American military center in England during World War II.

Often, the records found their way to a select group of fans who hung out in Liverpool's clubs and coffee bars. Liverpudlians—that is, Liverpool natives—were thus exposed to Elvis and performers like Jerry Lee Lewis, Little Richard, Chuck Berry, the Everly Brothers, Buddy Holly, and Bo Diddley long before the rest of England heard them.

A Meeting of the Minds

John and Paul met on July 6, 1957, at the annual fete (fair) sponsored by St. Peter's Parish Church in John's neighborhood, Woolton. The Quarrymen were part of

Invasion of the Teenagers

In this selection from his book Shout!, *writer Philip Norman sets the stage for the birth of John Lennon's first band in a depressed, dispirited England.*

"The year was one of unparalleled national humiliation. It was the year that the British engaged with France in a ludicrous plan to invade Egypt and were foiled by, of all people, the Egyptians. After Suez, the world would never again function at the behest of British gunboats. England had become overnight a second-class power, barely noticed in the new, harsh glare of America's and Russia's nuclear cohabitation.

The British language, meanwhile, had been invaded by certain bewildering new words. Of these, the most bewildering was 'teenager.' In Britain before 1956, there were no such things as teenagers. There were only children and grown-ups. Transition took place at sixteen when boys put on tweed jackets like their fathers' and girls turned into matrons with twinsets and perms. Conscription, or National Service, for two years, completed the male maturing process. The only remission was given to university students, a minority, still largely upper class, and thus permitted to behave like hooligans on Boat Race Night and other fixed ceremonial occasions."

Paul (pictured) was fourteen when he met John and was asked to join John's band. The two shared a love of American popular music, especially the music of Elvis Presley.

numbers like "Long Tall Sally," "Twenty Flight Rock," and "Tutti Frutti" proved he was a true connoisseur. John (who was nearsighted but vain about wearing glasses) paid the younger lad a compliment by sidling close enough to study his guitar technique: "I remember this beery old man," Paul once recalled, "getting nearer and breathing down me neck as I was playing."[8]

John wanted Paul, obviously the more talented guitarist of the two, to join the band, and a week later Paul was a Quarryman. He soon was asserting himself as strongly as John. Paul had no qualms about directing the others, telling them how he wanted them to sound. Also, he was as much a natural showman as John. They became close friends, especially after tragedy brought them even closer; a year after their first meeting, John's mother was killed by a speeding car. Paul had already survived the death of his mother and was able to help John deal with his grief.

In many ways, they were very different. John always spoke his mind and never hid his quick temper or contempt for authority. Paul's aggression and need for control were as strong as John's, but his personality was sunnier. John was quick to fight; Paul preferred to compromise. But their love of music kept them close, and although John was officially still the chief Quarryman, they soon developed a working dual leadership.

the day's entertainment; they played for free. Ivan Vaughan, a friend of Paul's and a sometime Quarryman, introduced them during a break in their performance.

John was a little drunk; at sixteen he was already fond of beer. As Pete Shotton recalled later, John and Paul were indifferent to each other when they first met: "Paul seemed quite cocky, sure of himself, but he and John didn't seem to have much to say."[7] John, for his part, ignored Paul, who was only fourteen. Soon, however, Paul proved himself worthy of notice by revealing a talent no Quarryman had: He knew how to tune a guitar.

Paul also had a knack for remembering song lyrics; John usually remembered only the first verse or two. Most impressive of all was Paul's taste—his love of obscure

George

Late in 1957, a friend of Paul's with jug ears and a shy smile began hanging around with the band. George Harrison,

George Harrison joined John's band, the Quarrymen, in 1958. George shared John and Paul's passion for American rock 'n' roll.

born on February 25, 1943, was a year behind Paul at the Liverpool Academy school. He was the fourth child of a bus driver, Harry Harrison, and his wife, Louise. Unlike John and Paul—and unlike Ringo, yet to join the band—he came from a relatively large family, lived with both parents, and had not suffered a difficult childhood. On the other hand, he resembled them in being a bright but rebellious working-class boy.

Like them, too, George was bitten hard by the rock 'n' roll bug. He had borrowed money from his mother for a guitar but soon realized that he did not have much natural ability. Things that other musicians could do with seeming ease required a lot of effort for George. Still, he

wanted to play. He sensed that he could learn through sheer hard work and stubbornness, and he set his strong will to the task.

Over the winter he began following the Quarrymen around, playing with them whenever he could. Another guitarist, Eric Griffiths, was in the band at the time. When George's ability began to surpass Griffiths's, in 1958, George was asked to replace him. The lineup now was John, Paul, and George on guitars, plus whoever they could get on drums; there was no bass player.

By this time the band was clearly headed away from skiffle. John, Paul, and George were by now playing electric guitars, though they couldn't afford amplifiers. If they were unable to borrow one for a gig, George (who was studying to become an electrician) would wire their instruments directly into whatever microphone system was available.

Along with the shift to rock 'n' roll came a new name. At the time, Britain was full of Elvis imitators with improbable handles like Marty Wilde, Dicky Pride, Duffy Power, and Vince Eager. Usually these singers were backed up by anonymous bands who got second billing. Liverpool's top band, for instance, was Rory Storm and the Hurricanes. The Quarrymen had two lead singers who were equal leaders, but they chose a conventional name for an audition in nearby Manchester: The Quar-rymen, which temporarily included drummer Colin Hanton, became Johnny and the Moondogs.

They didn't get the job, Hanton left the band, and for the rest of the year they performed only sporadically. John continued to attend art school on a scholarship; Paul kept up his studies to become a teacher; and George continued to be an apprentice electrician.

The Silver Beatles

In 1959, the band took in a new member. Stu Sutcliffe was a gifted painter with an

"Wonderfully Exuberant (and Somewhat Mindless)"

Writer Geoffrey Stokes, in this excerpt from his book The Beatles, *evokes the kind of music that inspired John and Paul and their cronies in the early days.*

"In 1958, the year George became a Quarryman, the charts overflowed with a wonderfully exuberant (and somewhat mindless) music that went right to the teenage heart. Buddy Holly had four songs—including 'Rave On' and 'Peggy Sue'—on the British charts that year; the Everly Brothers had two; Fats Domino, Little Richard and Jerry Lee Lewis, one apiece, and Elvis, six. But in that year a counterrevolution also began, as Cliff Richard, England's answer to Pat Boone, made the first of his many trips to the charts.

Without question, the Quarrymen knew which side they were on. They felt nothing but contempt for the polite, and ever-so religious, Richard. Rock 'n' roll—their music—wasn't polite, wasn't safe, wasn't anything the BBC's darling was. But that didn't stop them from stealing one of his band's riffs when Paul saw them play it on television, and this eclectic [wide-ranging] embrace of alien styles was to become a hallmark of the Beatles."

impressive intellect whom John had met at art school. John loved their long discussions about art and genius and rebellion. He urged Stu to join the band, and Stu was fascinated by the idea; playing in a band fit his self-image, and the fact that he had never played music didn't stop him. When he received an unexpectedly large sum of money for a painting, Stu spent it all on a bass guitar and joined up.

The Moondogs began playing semi-regularly at a coffee bar called the Jacaranda. The Jac, as it was known, had no mike stands. When the band played, fans would kneel in front of John and Paul to hold up hand mikes attached to mops. The club's owner, Allan Williams, arranged in 1960 for the band to audition for a choice engagement: backing up singer Billy Fury on tours of northern England and Scotland. One of Liverpool's top drummers, Johnny Hutch, agreed to

join them for the audition, although he didn't hide his opinion that the Moondogs "weren't worth a carrot."[9]

The audition prompted another name change. Stu came up with the Beetles in honor of Buddy Holly's band, the Crickets. Unable to resist a pun, John changed the spelling to reflect "beat music," a Liverpool term for rock 'n' roll. Inspired by Robert Louis Stevenson's *Treasure Island*, the band briefly called itself Long John and the Silver Beatles before settling on simply the Silver Beatles.

The Silver Beatles didn't pass the audition, but they did get another gig: backing up a minor singer, Johnny Gentle, on a two-week tour of Scotland. The pay was thirty-six pounds each. It was terrible money, but John, Paul, George, and Stu were thrilled at the prospect of playing outside Liverpool. They asked drummer Tommy Moore to join them. Moore, at thirty-six roughly twice the age of the

"At Least We Were Getting Famous"

George Harrison here recalls the band's first tour outside Liverpool, a two-week trip to Scotland. The quote is from Nicholas Schaffner's The Beatles Forever.

"At least we were getting famous, except it made us realise we didn't have any clothes. We looked a funny lot of buggers. We were dead rough and we were lucky to be there really, even though it wasn't very much. We travelled by van and you know there was a lot of fighting in those days, fighting for your inch. That's another thing. There's always fighting for your own space, even if it's only an inch. 'Give us the credit for having an inch.' So there was always a lot of that going on. That is why bands who make it rich quickly are quicker to get their own limousine."

When Stu Sutcliffe joined the band in 1959, he had never played a musical instrument.

others, made good money driving a forklift at a bottling company, but the others convinced him to take time off for the tour.

The Scottish tour was rough. When not playing, the musicians shared cramped quarters, ate rushed meals, and squeezed into a tiny van with their gear. The equipment was so cheap that when they played loudly the bass drum fell away from Moore's kit and went rolling across the stage. Moore hated the tour and quit the band immediately afterward to return to his forklift. For the others, Scotland had been rough but exhilarating; they'd had a taste of how real musicians lived and they wanted more.

Back in Liverpool, the drummerless band got its first steady gig: backing up strippers at a club Allan Williams owned. It was a pretty awful job, and it looked for a time as though the band was going nowhere. Then Germany beckoned.

2 Hamburg and the Cavern Club

It was Hamburg . . . where we really developed. To get the Germans going and keep it up for twelve hours at a time, we really had to hammer.

—John Lennon

Hamburg was in many ways the German equivalent to Liverpool: a bustling port, a rough-and-ready blue-collar town, and a cold northern environment. Several Liverpool bands had already gone there to satisfy the German craving for American-style rock 'n' roll. After Allan Williams heard glowing reports about Hamburg

from these bands, he decided the time was right for him to book a group there himself.

The promoter approached two other bands before he offered the gig to the Silver Beatles, but Rory Storm and the Hurricanes were already committed to another engagement and Gerry and the Pacemakers didn't want to go overseas. So the Silver Beatles, still without a drummer and still very raw, were booked into the Indra Club in Hamburg for a two-month engagement in the summer of 1960.

Paul McCartney and John Lennon team up with an unknown guitarist at the Casbah Club in Liverpool. Despite their inexperience and lack of a drummer, the band was booked for a gig in Germany in 1960.

"A Yin and Yang Thing"

In this excerpt from Yesterday, *a book about Paul McCartney, writer Chet Flippo reflects on the need for audience approval, a British music-hall tradition that McCartney inherited from his father.*

"Without an audience, [Paul] did not really exist. With one, he became almost superhuman. It was the big difference between him and John. Paul had to have that fix that an audience's attention and applause provided him. John began to shrink from it, as if he wasn't worthy of an audience's approval and applause. And if he wasn't worthy of it, then any scumbag audience that would offer him that was obviously . . . beneath even *his* contempt. And that became obvious even then. It was a yin and yang thing. John harangued and abused the audiences, rebuked them and scorned them, and then silver-tongued Paul came along to woo them and wow them, seduce them and bow to them, and to show that the whole Beatle act really was just an act and that the Beatles really did love you. Even on those days when John was at his most vicious and drunk and spaced out on amphetamines and he really meant what he said, Paul was usually able to gloss over it and the whole thing became an act.

Even the songs they were writing then and over the next couple of years showed that essential Beatle split: John's songs were invariably first-person songs, lyrics of introspection, of self-absorption, personal songs. Paul wrote mostly third-person songs, where he stepped outside himself and commented on others. No gut-spilling for Paul, unlike John. Paul became a control freak early on and John started going in the other direction almost as a reaction to that. But, again, that's where they would complement each other."

Aunt Mimi didn't like the idea of John missing so much school, but John was already failing and he was determined to go. Stu was more committed to his studies and balked at going, but John talked him into it. Paul convinced his father to let him go before starting teacher's college. And George met with little opposition; his parents had always encouraged his music. His mother even baked a tin of biscuits (cookies) to take on the trip, about which the others teased him mercilessly.

They still needed a drummer who could handle a two-month engagement. They found one at the Casbah, a tiny basement club where they sometimes played; in fact, he was the son of the woman who ran the place. Pete Best didn't smile or talk much—and he wasn't a very good drummer—but he was handsome and popular with the girls. Besides, Pete owned his own drum kit—a rare commodity among Liverpool's impoverished rock 'n' roll musicians.

In August 1960 Allan Williams drove the band to Hamburg in an old minibus. They squeezed in along with Williams's wife, his brother-in-law, his business partner, and even a German waiter who was taking a new job as interpreter for the Hamburg club owner who had hired the band. None of the musicians had a work permit; Williams told them that if asked about visas they were merely students on vacation.

Life in the Reeperbahn

The five teenagers were amazed, excited, and shocked at the first sight of their new home. The Reeperbahn neighborhood of Hamburg was (and still is) a rough area that catered to sailors on leave. It provided a wide variety of entertainment, much of it X-rated and all of it eye-opening to a group of inexperienced boys from the north of England. The Freiheit section of the Reeperbahn, where the Indra Club was located, was one of its roughest parts.

The band's new job hardly typified the glamorous life they might have imagined. The quarters provided by the club owner consisted of a filthy nest above a movie house. Paul remarked when he saw his tiny room, "You could just about swing a cat in here, providing it's got no tail!"[10] The only way to wash up was in the men's room of the theater. The Indra Club itself was a dingy basement joint, and the band was expected to play long sets every night: four and a half hours on weeknights and six on weekends. To top it off, their audiences were mostly prostitutes and their clients.

On the other hand, they liked much of what they saw. There was no shortage of German beer or willing German girls—especially the waitresses at the Indra. There was also a steady supply of diet pills called Preludins, amphetamines that kept them alert for hours. The only thing that was lacking was enough time for all the partying. As writer Philip Norman puts it, "The Freiheit provided an abundance of everything but sleep."[11]

So long as they did what the club's owner instructed—"Make show!"—they were free to perform however they liked. George continued to studiously apply himself to his solos, Stu remained passive behind his dark glasses, and Pete was always coolly sullen at his drums. It was John and Paul, of course, who made show. It became a game, trying desperately to outdo each other every night.

They would do anything to get a reaction. Paul might launch into a fullthroated, screaming Little Richard imitation or Elvis-style hip wiggling; John might appear onstage with a toilet seat around his neck or spew insults into the mike, calling the German audiences Nazis and worse. The crowd loved their antics and cheered for more. As John later put it, "We'd try anything we could think of because there was nobody to copy. So we played what we liked and the Germans liked it, too, as long as it was loud."[12]

Soon the band had attracted a steady crowd. The club's owner extended their contract and moved them to a bigger club, the Kaiserkeller. There they alternated shows with another band from Liverpool—Rory Storm and the Hurricanes. The Silver Beatles made particular friends with the drummer for the Hurricanes, a sad-eyed, bearded young man named Richard Starkey who used the stage name Ringo Starr. Ringo's nickname came from his habit of wearing large, gaudy rings on every finger. John, Paul, George, and Stu liked Ringo. His cheerful nature and quick wit were closer to their own style than that of Pete Best.

They made another connection at this time that would eventually become impor-

tant. Klaus Voorman was a shy art student who wanted to become an album designer. He wandered into a Silver Beatles performance one night and was immediately attracted to their rough music, wild stage presence, and leather-jacketed, greasy-haired style. Klaus and his girlfriend, a photographer named Astrid Kirchherr, became regulars at the Kaiserkeller. Soon, Stu and Astrid fell deeply in love; Klaus managed to remain friends with the band even after Astrid left him.

The Cavern Club

Near the end of the year the band secretly arranged to move to a rival club, the Top Ten, where they were offered better pay

Just "Making Show"

This description of one of the band's first appearances in the Liverpool area after their trip to Hamburg is from Chet Flippo's book Yesterday. *The expression "make show" refers to how the band imitated the German club manager's urgings to create a wild presence on stage.*

"There were perhaps fifteen hundred dancers on the floor in Litherland that night when the Beatles took the stage and Paul ripped into 'Long Tall Sally.' All those hours onstage in Hamburg paid off in one hell of a hurry. The musical urgency and authoritative beat these Beatles were laying down, along with their 'We don't give a damn' stage presence, was electrifying. The dancers rushed the stage—unheard of at a dance! They swarmed the stage, jumping up and down, yelling, screaming. . . . Girls went crazy; guys went nuts. It was a near-riot. The Beatles looked at each other, puzzled, uncomprehending at first. All they were doing was their German 'make show,' after all."

and working conditions. Unfortunately, when Pete and Paul snuck into their apartment to remove their things, Paul lit a match to see in a dark hallway. A curtain caught fire and they were arrested for trying to burn the building down. During the investigation, German authorities discovered that George was underage—he was seventeen—and none of the Beatles had a valid work permit. The band was ordered to return to Liverpool.

Back home, the boys found that things had changed for the better. Rock 'n' roll had caught on in a big way, and there were plenty of places to play. They began appearing regularly at local dances, with Pete Best's mother acting as their manager. They were usually billed as coming "Direct from Hamburg!!!," which gave them an exotic quality; Liverpool audiences were often amazed to discover that the band members spoke English.

They were still just Liverpool scruffs, but something was different about them now. In part it was a name change: After Hamburg the Silver Beatles had become simply the Beatles. In part it was the look; their greasy hair, black leather jackets, and cowboy boots set the Beatles apart from typical bands who trimmed their hair close and wore neat matching suits.

More importantly, their sound was different. Before their trip abroad, they had been just one group out of dozens in town, and they had been by no means the best. But Hamburg turned them into a tight, rocking unit that knew how to put on a show. John and Paul had improved as singers, and the unusual lineup of two lead voices singing in close harmony, with George adding a third vocal, added to

their appeal; virtually all the other bands relied on a single vocalist. Now they drew enthusiastic crowds, who followed them from dance to dance.

Shortly after the beginning of 1961, Mona Best talked the owner of a popular club into trying out her son's band. The Cavern Club was a dingy, windowless basement—little more than a long tunnel that smelled of sweat, beer, and food—but it was always jammed with teenagers who came to dance, drink Cokes, and eat cheese rolls.

The Beatles first played there as guests of the house band in March 1961. The large crowd they attracted cheered them on and ignored the regular band. The Cavern's owner offered to hire the Beatles to play daily at lunchtime. They nearly turned him down when he said they would have to wear suits, but the club's DJ convinced them it was worth the sacrifice and they signed on.

The Beatles at this point were not much more than a talented cover band. Their repertoire at the Cavern Club consisted almost entirely of songs by American R&B, rock 'n' roll, and country singers. For variety, they also played old songs like "Besame Mucho" or ballads from Broadway musicals (one of which, "Till There Was You," would show up on an early Beatles album). John and Paul had begun writing songs together, but they were still self-conscious about their own material.

Hamburg Again

In the spring of 1961 the band returned to the Top Ten Club in Hamburg for

The Beatles play at the Cavern Club, a popular teen hangout in Liverpool. The photo reveals the band's new look—greasy hair and leather jackets. The band had also improved musically.

three months. This time they made the arrangements themselves—and they had valid working permits.

Stu Sutcliffe had been waffling about quitting the band. He wanted to concentrate on his painting and was embarrassed at his lack of musical ability. He couldn't sing and had never been a good bassist— he often turned his back on the audience to hide the fact that he could barely play. Paul, the most accomplished musician in the group, was openly contemptuous of Stu's failings.

Paul kept saying that he, Paul, should be the one playing bass. John knew that Paul was right, but John was also loyal to

his art-school friend. In the end, Stu left the group, won a scholarship to a prestigious Hamburg art school, and moved into a room in Astrid's family home. Paul traded in his guitar for a bass, and the band became a quartet.

In May, the Top Ten's other act, a Liverpudlian named Tony Sheridan, recorded for the German label Polydor. The Beatles, identified on the label as "the Beat Brothers," played backup. The tunes included "My Bonnie," a rocking version of the old standby "My Bonnie Lies over the Ocean," a familiar melody to German audiences. It was released as a single the following month.

"We Would Do the Same"

In this excerpt from Hunter Davies' official Beatles biography, The Beatles, *George Harrison recalls the glory days of Liverpool's Cavern Club.*

"We probably loved the Cavern best of anything. It was fantastic. We never lost our identification with the audience all the time. We never rehearsed anything, not like the other groups who kept on copying the Shadows. We were playing to our own fans who were like us. They would come in their lunchtimes to hear us and bring their sandwiches to eat instead of having lunch. We would do the same, eating our lunch while we played. The audience sat there and ate while we stood up there and ate as we played. We enjoyed it all and so did they. It was just spontaneous. Everything just happened."

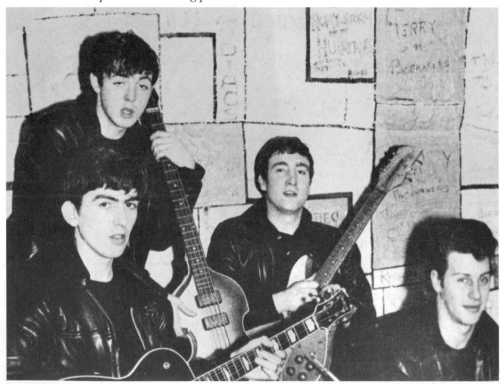

(From left to right) George, Paul, John, and Pete Best onstage at the Cavern Club. Playing at the Cavern would prove a launching point in their career.

The early Beatles, Pete, George, John, and Paul, on their way to fame. After proving themselves in Hamburg and gaining popularity back in Liverpool, the Beatles wanted to go beyond their regional fame.

That summer the band, minus Stu, returned to Liverpool. Back home, the Beatles began playing the Cavern again, this time for more prestigious and better-paying evening shows. By the fall they were the top band in the city.

Rock 'n' roll was so strong in Liverpool by now that a new newspaper was devoted to covering it: *Mersey Beat*, named in honor of the city's Mersey River. The Beatles were the stars of virtually every issue. They placed first in its popularity poll that year, in part because the Beatles themselves had shamelessly stuffed the ballot box. As Bill Harry, the paper's editor, recalled:

There were enough legitimate votes from the girls to assure the Beatles first place. I could recognize the writing of most group members and really didn't count those [ballots] sent in bundles with the same handwriting.[13]

Hamburg had toughened the Beatles and made them professionals, and they were enjoying the regional fame that came with success. But they wanted more than simply to be the top band in their hometown. Within a year, their wish would come true.

3 Becoming Famous

Sorry, Mr. Epstein, but groups with guitars are on their way out.

—Dick Rowe of Decca Records, turning down the Beatles for a recording contract in early 1962

Brian Epstein first heard about the Beatles in the fall of 1961. Customers were coming into his Liverpool record shop asking about "My Bonnie," the record on which "The Beat Brothers" backed Tony Sheridan. Anyone who read *Mersey Beat* knew the real identity of the band, and Liverpool's music fans were eager to hear their favorite group's debut.

Epstein's father ran a successful chain of stores, North End Music Stores (NEMS), that sold furniture, pianos, radios, and record players. As a teenager Brian had wanted to become a dress designer or an actor, but he had bowed to family pressure, joined his father's business, and expanded one shop to include a record department.

In the fall of 1961 Brian was twenty-seven, much older than the teenaged Beatles and their fans. He had always cultivated an air of suave sophistication, and he personally preferred classical composers to pop music. But like any good businessman he paid attention to his customers. When he was unable to order

copies of "My Bonnie," he decided to track it down himself.

Brian knew from *Mersey Beat* (in which he wrote a record column and took out advertising space) that the Beatles were performing at the Cavern Club, and in early November he dropped by. He hated the club's crowded, overheated atmosphere. In his memoirs, *A Cellarful of Noise*, he writes, "Inside the club it was as black as a deep grave, dank and damp and smelly, and I regretted my decision to come."[14]

"Right Then, Brian. Manage Us."

But something fascinated him about the scruffy, wisecracking, leather-clad musicians onstage. He liked them immediately, and for the rest of his life the Beatles remained Brian Epstein's great obsession. Some Beatles biographers have argued that Epstein, who was gay, was physically attracted to them, especially John. But Epstein's interest involved something other than a sexual attraction; to him the Beatles represented an exciting, unfamiliar new world.

Brian longed for glamour and refinement. He wanted to escape the confines of his stuffy family business and of Liverpool's provincial, middle-class values. His dream was to live in a world where the fact that he was Jewish would not matter, and—since homosexuality was illegal in England in the 1960s—where he would not have to hide his sex life. In short, he was bored and frustrated; as he soon found out, so were the Beatles, and he sensed that the band could be his ticket to new adventures.

After several more visits to the Cavern Club, Epstein arranged to meet the band and began formulating a plan to become their manager. He had never managed an act before, but he consulted colleagues in the music business and learned how the system operated. At the end of November, he asked the Beatles to meet with him and nervously laid out his management plans.

The Beatles were amused and surprised that a well-off, older businessman would be interested in them. But they were also frustrated at the slow pace of their career, and they were willing to listen to him. Their only major question was whether Epstein expected them to change their music. When he said no, they were quiet for a long time. John Lennon finally broke the silence by saying briskly, "Right then, Brian. Manage us."[15]

At first, the partnership did not seem promising. The first booking Epstein arranged for the band was in a local café. After paying for posters and gasoline for the band's borrowed van, they made a profit of exactly one pound. Gradually, however, the gigs began to improve.

The band began to change its image. The neat, well-groomed Epstein convinced the Beatles that to succeed they needed to be more presentable. His new rules included no more showing up late or drunk; no talking to friends or joking privately onstage; no more eating or drinking while playing; and absolutely no belching into the microphones.

Brian got them stylish new gray suits and even made them smoke a new brand of cigarette: sophisticated Senior Services instead of the working-class Woodbines they were used to. Paul enjoyed this new image makeover; Pete and George were less enthusiastic but went along with it. John, always the rebel, complained loudly but eventually agreed.

One crucial change in the Beatles' look came not from Epstein but from

Brian Epstein, manager of the Beatles. Epstein was largely responsible for what became the Beatles' new look—their collarless suits and more clean-cut image.

their Hamburg friend Astrid Kirchherr. Back in Germany, Astrid had styled Stu's hair so that it fell forward in bangs across his forehead, rather than sweeping back in a greasy pompadour. At first the other Beatles had mocked the new hairdo, but they came to like it and all of them adopted it—with the exception of Pete, who kept his short and swept back. In time, Astrid's work would become the most famous hairstyle in the world.

A Recording Contract at Last

Within weeks of becoming the Beatles' manager, Epstein began making the rounds of London's record labels in search of a contract. His first experiences were solid rejections by virtually every company.

In the meantime, the band returned to Hamburg for an engagement at its biggest nightspot, the Star-Club. Astrid met them with shocking news: Stu Sutcliffe, who had been experiencing headaches and blackouts, had died of a brain hemorrhage. The cause was unclear. It is possible the hemorrhage was caused by a head wound received in one of the Beatles' many fights with rowdy club patrons.

This tragic news was offset somewhat by a telegram from Brian Epstein: "Congratulations, boys. EMI request recording session. Please rehearse new material."[16]

It had been an uphill battle for Brian. He was convinced that his new clients would someday be bigger than Elvis, however, and his enthusiasm prevailed. The telegram he sent to Hamburg, typical of this enthusiasm, was misleading. The gig was just an audition, not a full recording session; and the label was Parlophone, a tiny branch of the much larger EMI record company.

Still, it was great news, if for no other reason than the fact that it marked the beginning of the Beatles' relationship with the other person besides Brian Epstein who would have a huge influence on the band's success and growth—producer George Martin. Martin was the head of A&R at Parlophone. A&R stands for "artist and repertoire"; A&R departments find and foster new talent. Parlophone was the poor sister of the EMI group, with no hits to its credit. The label's reputation lay in comedy, light orchestral, and spoken-word records.

George Martin was a skilled musician and composer, but in early 1962 he was best known as the producer of the Goons, a British comedy troupe that included actor Peter Sellers. Eager to score a hit in the pop music market, he was open to new sounds. He was only mildly interested in the tape that Brian Epstein first played him; as the producer recalled later, "The recording, to put it mildly, was by no means a knock-out." It was made up of old songs like "Ain't She Sweet" and "Your Feet's Too Big," which Epstein thought would attract more attention than original compositions. Martin didn't like the corny material, but he was intrigued with what he called an "unusual quality of sound, a certain roughness that I hadn't encountered before."[17]

He also liked the fact that three of the Beatles sang; this was a group effort, rather than the more usual solo act with backup. And so in March 1962, the band entered EMI's studios in Abbey Road. They recorded, strictly as a test, a number

"Teenager's Turn"

In his book Yesterday, *Chet Flippo describes an important moment in the band's rise to national prominence.*

"A major obstacle fell on March 7, 1962, at 8 P.M. when the Beatles recorded their first BBC radio show. Brian had gotten them an audition with the BBC on February 12 and they had, typically, charmed Peter Pilbeam, the producer of the show *Teenager's Turn (Here We Go)*. On that day, after hearing John and Paul both sing, Pilbeam wrote on his audition notes: JOHN LENNON, YES. PAUL MCCARTNEY, NO. He later reconsidered his judgment.

The first show was taped before an audience at the Playhouse Theatre in Manchester and was broadcast on March 8 at 5 P.M. For the taping John sang lead on 'Hello Little Girl,' 'Memphis,' and 'Please Mr. Postman' and Paul sang 'Dream Baby (How Long Must I Dream?),' the Roy Orbison song that Paul had done at the audition. ('Hello Little Girl,' the only Lennon-McCartney song they did, was dropped from the broadcast.)

This was the first of more than fifty BBC appearances by the Beatles. (They started calling it the Beatles Broadcasting Corporation.) Said Pilbeam: 'I was very impressed with them and I booked them straightaway for another date after that first show.'"

of old standards as well as originals such as "Love Me Do" and "P.S. I Love You."

Martin liked what he heard and offered the Beatles a one-year contract. He agreed to record four titles during that time. In return, they and their manager would get one penny per record sold, to be divided among them all. It was not much of a contract from the band's perspective, but Martin was their last hope. They had already been turned down by virtually every other record executive in London.

Besides, they liked Martin. The tall, calm, impeccably mannered, schoolmasterish Martin and the scruffy, teenaged, wisecracking Beatles had hit it off immediately. The band was thrilled at Martin's connection with the Goons, great heroes of the smart-mouthed musicians. (On *The Beatles Live at the BBC*, early recordings released in 1994, John can be heard imitating some of the manic voices Peter Sellers used as a Goon.) More importantly, Martin was immediately straightforward and honest with them.

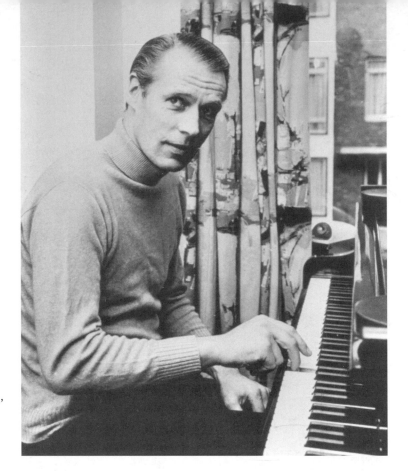

George Martin produced the Beatles' first records. Martin liked both the Beatles' music and their hip, sarcastic manner.

In turn, the producer was charmed by the Beatles' personalities and humor. Especially their humor. In his memoirs and interviews, Martin has stressed repeatedly that the Beatles won their contract as much for their funny, endearing ways as for their musical ability.

Exit Pete, Enter Ringo

Martin was not happy with Pete Best's drumming and told Epstein he would use a professional studio drummer for recording, though it didn't matter to him if Pete played on live dates. But the pressure to drop Best had been mounting for some

time; the other Beatles, dissatisfied with Pete's musicianship and personality, had never considered him a permanent member. Martin's comment was the final straw in their decision to fire him.

John, Paul, and George asked Brian in August to give Pete the news; they didn't want to do it themselves. Best took a job as a baker in Liverpool and tried to make a career in music for himself, but he soon faded into obscurity. Pete's replacement, meanwhile, was just what the band needed—the missing part that completed the puzzle. He was none other than the sad-eyed drummer the band had befriended in Hamburg.

Richard Starkey, the oldest Beatle, was born on July 7, 1940. His father left early on; young Ritchie was raised by his mother, a barmaid, and his grandfather, a shipyard laborer. Ritchie was a sickly child and missed school often. Even as a teenager he could read and write only with difficulty, and his hair was already beginning to turn gray from ill health. He worked as a messenger, barman, and shipyard laborer while drumming on weekends, but his natural ability soon led him to full-time musicianship. By the time he first met the Beatles in Hamburg, Ringo was a seasoned professional and far more experienced than John, Paul, or George.

In August 1962, after Ringo had been with Rory Storm's band for four years, two interesting offers came his way. One was from Liverpool singer King-Size Taylor at twenty pounds a week; the other was from the Beatles, who offered him

Completing the Jigsaw

This excerpt from Brian Epstein's memoirs, A Cellarful of Noise, *describes Ringo Starr's entry into the band. It glosses over the firing of Pete Best by referring to his "disappearance" as if the rest of the band had nothing to do with it.*

"I have known them [the Beatles] so long, so well and with such personal involvement that I rarely try to examine what has happened or why. I was there when the foursome was born—when the face of Ringo slotted into the curious chemical pattern and thus created the four-constituent formula which has driven the young womanhood of the world into a demented frenzy of exultation and admiration.

Yet I cannot pretend that, facially, Ringo seemed to me to be the perfect fit. And certainly the other three did not band together originally because they knew that somehow they were to become a hypnotic blend. George and Paul and John linked up simply because they were three teenagers keen on making music and because they could do it without rowing or arguing over small things.

In other words they got on well together, and when the disappearance of Pete Best left them without a drummer, they asked for Ringo because he could do the job and because they liked him. But . . . it is inescapable that Ringo was the catalyst for the others. He certainly completed the jigsaw and the Beatles with Ringo became a magnet for the great camera-artists of the world, a target for the jaded lately hostile eyes of people who had hardly known that popular music existed."

Re-Creating Live Performance

In Gareth L. Pawlowski's book about the band's early days, How They Became the Beatles, *the band's first recording engineer, Norman Smith, describes making the first Beatles album.*

"The whole idea was just to let them record numbers exactly as they've been doing onstage. I added to the performance feel in the studio by positioning them much as they are onstage, with Ringo and his drums at the back, then George in front of him, and Paul and John in the center doing their vocals.

The main things I remember were a large tin of Hack cough sweets which were stuck into a handy position on the piano, so that Paul and John could dig into it whenever they wanted to, and a couple of cartons of Peter Stuyvesant cigarettes that they steadily worked through during the day.

The boys were very, very happy when they heard the playback at the end of the day."

The Beatles, now complete with Ringo, during a 1964 recording session.

As one writer commented, when Ringo Starr joined the Beatles in 1962, he "fit in like a missing tooth."

twenty-five pounds a week. Ringo opted for the better pay.

The Liverpool fans were outraged at the switch. They signed petitions, kept all-night vigils outside Pete Best's home, and even started fistfights; publicity photos from this period show George in profile to hide a black eye. Ringo himself wasn't sure at the time that the switch was for the best. He later said:

The birds [girls] loved Pete. Me, I was just a skinny, bearded scruff. Brian

didn't really want me either. He thought I didn't have the personality. And why get a bad-looking cat when you can get a good-looking one?[18]

But the change made all the difference. With Ringo, the Beatles became a powerful entity—not just a great rock 'n' roll band but a perfect blend of personalities. As writer Chet Flippo remarked about Ringo, "once he sat down behind John, Paul, and George, he fit in like a missing tooth."[19] It was all they needed to conquer England.

4 Capturing England

If the Beatles made a disc of themselves snoring for two minutes, it'd go to Number One!

—British disc jockey Brian Matthew, August 1963

In September 1962, the Beatles traveled to London for their first full recording session under their own name. As with the earlier audition, the location was EMI's studio in Abbey Road. George Martin started by giving the nervous band a tour of the studio, explaining each part of the recording procedure, and urging them to ask questions. He ended by telling them to let him know if there was anything they didn't like. George grinned and said, "Well, for a start, I don't like your tie."[20]

The remark cracked everyone up, including the normally reserved Martin. The other Beatles acted as though George had done something naughty in school, punching him playfully on the shoulders as if he were a student who had talked back. Any tension the band felt in the unfamiliar surroundings dissolved, and for the rest of the day their wisecracks kept Martin and his engineer, Norman Smith, helpless with laughter.

Martin chose two Lennon-McCartney originals from the songs the band played for him: "Love Me Do" would be the main side of the band's first single and "P.S. I Love You" would be the flip side. In fact, two versions of "Love Me Do" were recorded.

Until that day, Martin didn't know that Ringo had replaced Pete Best. The producer had already asked an experienced studio drummer, Andy White, to be present. Martin was unwilling to take a chance on the unknown Ringo, and he decided to keep White. Ringo was so unhappy that Martin said he would tape two versions of "Love Me Do," one with White and one with Ringo. Whichever version was better would be released.

According to Martin's memoirs, Ringo's version is probably the one that was released, although no one bothered to note it at the time. There was no more question about replacing Ringo. The producer realized that Ringo was very capable and that his loose, distinctive sound added to the recording. "You can tell Ringo's drums from anyone else's," Martin once noted, "and that character was a definite asset to the Beatles' early recordings."[21]

Everyone was pleased with the recordings, and Martin released the single in early October. Other executives at EMI were skeptical; American musicians so dominated the British record charts that the chances for an obscure group from a backwater British city were slim—

especially since EMI was giving the band little publicity.

Epstein solved the problem by ordering ten thousand copies for his record shop. This ensured that the record would at least make it onto the sales charts. The strategy worked; the single remained on the charts long enough for it to catch on by itself. By mid-December it had risen to number seventeen on the chart kept by the British music paper *New Musical Express.*

"Please Please Me"

For the follow-up single, Martin was enthused about a song called "How Do You Do It?" by a writer named Mitch Murray. But Paul and John hated the tune and insisted on recording another original. Martin replied that when they wrote hit material they could record it; until then, they should do what he said. The band retaliated by playing a deliberately terrible version of "How Do You Do It?"—so bad that it could never be released.

Martin backed down and agreed to record their song "Please Please Me." He helped them revise and strengthen the arrangement, and the band needed only one take to record a strong version. The producer was so satisfied with this take that he pressed the intercom between the recording booth and the control room and announced, "Gentlemen, you've just made your first number-one record."[22]

Martin was right. The record was released in mid-January and by March it was on top of the charts.

The record's turning point came when Epstein arranged an appearance in mid-January on a popular Saturday night TV variety show, *Thank Your Lucky Stars.* The broadcast coincided with the worst storm England had suffered in years; virtually the entire nation was at home watching "the telly," and an estimated 6 million of them saw the Beatles.

George Martin collaborates with the Beatles during a recording session. Martin had discouraged the Beatles from playing original songs—until the Lennon-McCartney song "Please Please Me" hit number one.

They caused quite a stir. For one thing, they didn't look like a normal pop group. The long hair was unusual. So were the instruments: John strummed an acoustic guitar and Paul's bass was oddly shaped and upside down. Instead of looking earnest and serious like most bands, the musicians grinned as they played. Strangest of all, the audience was screaming nonstop—a shocking thing for normally reserved Britons to witness. The music itself was barely noticed.

The *Thank Your Lucky Stars* appearance generated interest among England's press, and reporters discovered how witty the band was. A reporter would ask, "Are those wigs you're wearing?" and Ringo would reply, "If they are, they must be the only wigs with dandruff." "What kind of guitar is that, Paul?" someone else would ask, and the instrument would suddenly be tossed in the reporter's lap. "It's a Hofner violin bass. Here, take a look." "Are they expensive?" "Fifty-six

Outstanding Composers

Classical music critic William Mann, writing in the Times of London, *in late 1963, was one of the first mainstream commentators to approve of Beatlemania. This excerpt is reprinted in* The Lennon Companion.

"The outstanding English composers of 1963 must seem to have been John Lennon and Paul McCartney, the talented young musicians from Liverpool whose songs have been sweeping the country since last Christmas, whether performed by their own group, The Beatles, or by the numerous other teams of English troubadours that they also supply with songs. . . .

For several decades, in fact since the decline of the music-hall, England has taken her popular songs from the United States, either directly or by mimicry. But the songs of Lennon and McCartney are distinctly indigenous [native] in character, the most imaginative and inventive examples of a style that has been developing on Merseyside during the past few years. And there is a nice, rather flattering irony in the news that The Beatles have now become prime favourites in America too. . . .

One wonder[s] with interest what The Beatles, and particularly Lennon and McCartney, will do next, and if America will spoil them or hold on to them, and if their next record will wear as well as the others. They have brought a distinctive and exhilarating flavour into a genre of music that was in danger of ceasing to be music at all."

guineas. I could afford a better one but I'm a skinflint."[23]

After the flurry of publicity, EMI began promoting the new single and by early March it hit number one.

The First LP

In the early days of playing around Liverpool, the Beatles would pep themselves up with a group cheer. At odd moments John shouted, "Where are we going, fellas?" The others answered, "To the top, Johnny, to the top!" John yelled, "And where is the top, fellas?" Back came the answer: "To the toppermost of the poppermost!"[24]

Now they were on top. Everyone was ecstatic, but there was no time to celebrate. The band needed to follow their single quickly with a long-playing album; otherwise, they ran the risk of becoming one-hit wonders who would sink from sight. In February the band churned out the LP *Please Please Me* in a marathon sixteen-hour session squeezed into their hectic tour schedule.

Recording technology was far less sophisticated in the 1960s than today. *Please Please Me* was done in mono; stereo was known only to few audiophiles. Also, Abbey Road had machines that recorded only two tracks, unlike modern studios that routinely record twenty-four or more separate tracks. This meant the Beatles had no room for overdubbing, the layering on of extra vocal or instrumental tracks. They recorded all the instruments at once, playing more or less as they did live, then recorded vocals on the second track.

Martin extensively edited, shaped, and arranged the material, a mix of originals (like "I Saw Her Standing There") and cover versions of songs by American writers (notably "Twist and Shout" by the Isley Brothers). The producer also contributed occasionally himself on piano. Most of the lead vocals were by John and Paul, although George and Ringo each got one tune: George sang "Do You Want to Know a Secret?" in a thick Liverpudlian accent, and Ringo applied his limited but endearing voice to "Boys."

Music fans across England responded enthusiastically to the joy and good humor the band projected, and the album, released in March, was an even bigger success than the single for which it was named. It jumped to the top of the charts within seven weeks and stayed there for a record-breaking twenty-nine weeks. That spring and summer, the band made its first tours as headliners. They were astonished by the ecstatic crowds they encountered.

The Madding Crowd

Screaming crowds were not new in entertainment. In the previous century, thirty thousand cheering spectators turned out to greet the Swedish singer Jenny Lind when she docked in New York, and similar crowds greeted every stop of her American tour. Twenty years before the Beatles arrived, a skinny crooner of romantic ballads, Frank Sinatra, created a similar frenzy among teenagers. But nothing approached the intensity of the craziness that was forming around the Beatles.

The band was used to hometown fans rushing the stage, but it was not prepared for ecstatic receptions elsewhere. And yet here were fans lining up hours before the

"The Dull, the Idle"

Typical of adult reactions to Beatlemania was this excerpt from a piece by Paul Johnson in the New Statesman *in 1964, also reprinted in* The Lennon Companion.

"If The Beatles and their like were in fact what the youth of Britain wanted, one might well despair. I refuse to believe it—and so I think will any other intelligent person who casts his or her mind back far enough. . . . At 16, I and my friends heard our first performance of Beethoven's Ninth Symphony; I can remember the excitement even today. We would not have wasted 30 seconds of our precious time on The Beatles and their ilk.

Are teenagers different today? Of course not. Those who flock round The Beatles, who scream themselves into hysteria, whose vacant faces flicker over the TV screen, are the least fortunate of their generation, the dull, the idle, the failures: their existence, in such large numbers . . . is a fearful indictment of our education system, which in 10 years of schooling can scarcely raise them to literacy. [T]he core of the teenage group—the boys and girls who will be the real leaders and creators of society tomorrow—never go near a pop concert. They are, to put it simply, too busy. They are educating themselves. They are in the process of inheriting the culture which, despite Beatlism or any other mass-produced mental opiate, will continue to shape our civilisation."

shows, screaming nonstop from the moment the band hit the stage, even mobbing their car afterward. No longer could the band walk the streets in peace; now the only time they went outside was to shuttle between hotel and auditorium by car. They never saw the towns they played. Often, the hotel kitchen was closed by the time the Beatles finished their show; many of their meals consisted of cold cereal.

Avoiding crowds was a constant problem, and narrow escapes were common.

Once they escaped by running from the theater to the fire station next door, then leaving in a police car while a fire truck created a diversion by roaring away in the opposite direction. A hefty Cavern Club bouncer, Mal Evans, was hired as a bodyguard. Evans joined a support team that already included Epstein; Neil Aspinall, the Beatles' longtime driver and assistant; and London music writer Tony Barrow, now a full-time publicity man for Epstein's NEMS Enterprises.

Writing Together

Although they had been reluctant to play them in public at first, Lennon and McCartney had been writing songs together since the very beginning. Their different temperaments and styles made them an excellent writing team.

John's aggression was held back by Paul's sense of politeness; Paul's sentimentality was checked by John's cynicism. Either one could go overboard if left alone: John had a tendency to lecture in his songs; Paul had a tendency to be tedious or silly. Together, however, their differences complemented each other perfectly. John once commented, "My contribution was always to add a little bluesy edge to [the songs]. He provided a lightness, an optimism, while I would always go for the sadness, the discords, the bluesy notes."[25]

Usually, one would half finish a song and then ask the other for help in polishing it. Whoever wrote most of a tune usually sang lead. Often their best songs were written under the pressure of time deadlines in cramped dressing rooms, vans, or hotel rooms.

A good example was "She Loves You." Paul and John needed to produce a new single quickly; Paul had the seed of an idea for a call-and-response song in which one singer replies to what the other has just sung, a musical form that R&B had borrowed from American gospel singing. McCartney recalled later:

> John and I agreed it was a pretty crummy idea as it stood and since we were borrowing an American thing, I suppose it was crummy. But at least we had the basic idea of writing the song. That night in Newcastle we just sat in the hotel bedroom for a few hours and wrote it.[26]

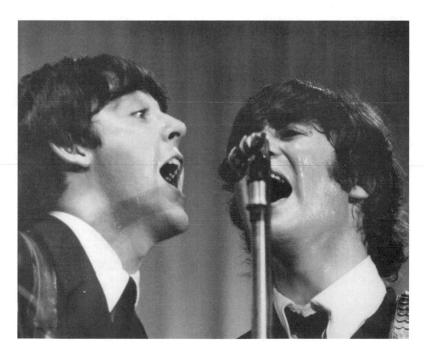

Paul and John sing vocals during a live performance. The two certainly rank among the most successful songwriting teams in history.

When they played the tune for Martin a few days later, the producer liked it but made a critical suggestion. He asked them to start the tune not with the verse—"Well, you think you've lost your love . . ."—but with its catchy chorus: "She loves you, yeah, yeah, yeah." This small alteration kicked the song into high gear; "yeah, yeah, yeah" soon became the Beatles' trademark and is still one of the best-known musical fragments in the world.

Scruffs No More

In part, the Beatles' fame continued to grow because of good timing. That summer two major embarrassments rocked England. One was the Profumo story, a steamy sex scandal that linked call girls with top government officials from Great Britain and the Soviet Union; the other was the Great Train Robbery, in which a gang of criminals escaped with a fortune and were taunting the once-invincible Scotland Yard. In the wake of these dispiriting stories, the Beatles fad was the perfect lightweight news story—newspapers eagerly reported its every twist and shout.

Their growing fame forced the band to give up some of the qualities that had first attracted Liverpool fans. No longer were they simple working-class scruffs like their fans; now they were stars. No longer were their performances casual affairs in tiny clubs; now they played short, controlled shows in big theaters. Some long-time Liverpool fans resisted buying the Beatles' records because they didn't want their heroes to get too popular, but most accepted the change. As one put it, "They were still our Beatles so far as the music

was concerned. . . . We didn't feel they were letting us down by leaving Liverpool, but things would never be the same."[27]

Meanwhile, the whole country was going Beatle crazy. Not everyone thought the Beatles were wonderful. A writer for the *Daily Telegraph*, for instance, claimed that the mass hysteria they created was filling empty heads just like Hitler had once done. Overall, though, it seemed as if everyone in England suddenly needed to know the tiniest detail about the four musicians. When a publisher of teen magazines proposed starting a monthly Beatles fan letter, a bewildered Paul asked him, "What are you going to find to write about us every month?"[28] The publisher replied that he would have no trouble finding enough material, and he didn't.

The country's infatuation continued into the fall. In September the music magazine *Melody Maker* announced that the Beatles were the top group in their annual poll. The London *Daily Mirror*, meanwhile, typified England's love affair with the band when it commented, "You have to be a real sour square not to love the nutty, noisy, happy, handsome Beatles. If they don't sweep your blues away, brother, you're a lost cause."[29]

But the price of fame, the Beatles were discovering, was to live life in a fishbowl. As the band became increasingly difficult to reach, reporters and fans began besieging the musicians' families. Their parents regularly chased away groups of girls who camped out on their doorsteps or tried to steal souvenirs from back kitchens.

Perhaps the worst off was Cynthia Lennon, who had married John the previous summer after becoming pregnant. Marriage was not part of the carefree Beatle image Brian Epstein wanted to present. The

"A Fresh Avalanche"

In his book Shout! *Philip Norman describes the enormous deluge of Beatle paraphernalia in England.*

"Christmas 1963 signaled a fresh avalanche of Beatle products into the shops. There were Beatle guitars, of plastic, authentically 'autographed,' and miniature Beatle drums. There were Beatle lockets, each with a tiny quadruple photograph compressed inside. There were red and blue Beatle kitchen aprons, bespeckled with guitar-playing bugs. The four faces and four signatures, engraved, printed or transferred, however indistinctly, appeared on belts, badges, handkerchieves, jigsaw puzzles, rubber airbeds, disc racks, bedspreads, ottomans, shoulder bags, pencils, buttons and trays. There was a brand of confectionery known as Ringo Roll, and of Beatle chewing gum, each sixpenny packet warranted to contain seven photographs. A northern bakery chain announced guitar shaped Beatle cakes ('Party priced at five shillings') and fivepenny individual Beatle 'fancies' [small cakes]."

Cardboard standups of the Beatles stand among a few of the spin-off products spawned by the band's popularity. These items are valuable collectibles today.

wedding was kept a secret and Cynthia was told to keep a low profile. After reporters discovered the truth, shy Cynthia and her baby, Julian, went from seclusion to life in a fishbowl. She recalled one especially rude reporter who discovered her shopping: "I managed to dart out the back of [the store] and into a fruit shop next door where I hid for half an hour till he'd gone."[30]

Playing for Royalty

In October the band was seen by its largest audience yet, some 15 million people, when it appeared on the nation's number-one TV variety show, *Sunday Night at the London Palladium.* That same month, Epstein's organization as well as Brian and the Beatles themselves moved to London. George and Ringo roomed together, John and Cynthia found an apartment, and Paul moved in with the family of his new girl-friend, a well-known actress named Jane Asher. This last move was kept secret; Brian still avoided any public perception that "the boys" might be other than squeaky clean.

Also in October, the band toured Sweden, its first trip outside England since Hamburg. On their return, hundreds of screaming girls were waiting at London's Heathrow airport. The fans caused such a commotion that the British prime minister and the newly elected Miss World, both of whom happened to be passing through the airport at the time, were completely ignored by the press.

In November the group released its second album, *With the Beatles.* It had been recorded in July, but Parlophone held off until the sales of the first LP began to drop. Like that summer's smash, "She Loves You," the group's Christmastime single, "I Want to Hold Your Hand," went instantly to number one.

Also in November, the Beatles appeared in the annual Command Variety

Paul with girlfriend Jane Asher.

The Beatles at the Command Variety Performance given for England's royal family. Their presence at the performance was an indication of their tremendous popularity.

Performance. This program for England's royal family is one of the most prestigious events a British entertainer can participate in. It was a great honor and an indication of their celebrity.

Queen Elizabeth was unable to be there, but the show was attended by both the Queen Mother and Princess Margaret, the queen's sister. The Beatles sang four songs to close the show. Just before the final number, "Twist and Shout," John Lennon stepped to the microphone and with a smile announced, "For this number we'd like to ask for your help. Will the people in the cheaper seats clap your hands? All the rest of you, just rattle your jewelry."[31]

John's cheeky remark became an instant legend and a symbol of the band's irreverent appeal. The Queen Mother remarked to reporters after the show that she liked the group very much. The next day's headlines said it all: BEATLES ROCK THE ROYALS. NIGHT OF TRIUMPH FOR FOUR YOUNG MEN. The headline in the *Daily Mirror* may have been the first public appearance of a phrase that would soon become commonplace; it simply read BEATLEMANIA![32]

By Christmas 1963 the Beatles were firmly on top in England. Their nonstop tour schedule was sold out. "I Want to Hold Your Hand" was number one. Six more singles from their second LP were in the top twenty, and the album itself was breaking

"Oh, We Like the Beatles"

This interview done in Paris just prior to the Beatles' invasion of America shows their wit, their confidence, their uncertainty about the future, and a rarely-heard-in-public flash of cynicism from John Lennon. It is reprinted in Geoffrey Giuliano's The Lost Beatles Interviews.

"QUESTION: How important is it to succeed here?

PAUL: It is important to succeed everywhere.

QUESTION: The French have not made up their minds about the Beatles. What do you think of them?

JOHN: Oh, we like the Beatles.

QUESTION: Do you like topless bathing suits?

RINGO: We've been wearing them for years.

QUESTION: Girls rushed toward my car because it had press identification and they thought I met you. How do you explain this phenomenon?

JOHN: You're lovely to look at.

QUESTION: What about your future?

RINGO: None of us has quite grasped what it is all about yet. It's washing over our heads like a huge tidal wave. But we're young. Youth is on our side. And it's youth that matters right now. I don't care about politics, just people.

GEORGE: I wouldn't do all this if I didn't like it. I wouldn't do anything I didn't want to, would I?

QUESTION: Is it true you're only in this for the money?

PAUL: Security is the only thing I want. Money to do nothing with, money to have in case you wanted to do something.

JOHN: People say we're loaded with money, but by comparison with those who are supposed to talk the Queen's English that's ridiculous. We're only earning. They've got real capital behind them and they're earning on top of that. The more people you meet, the more you realize it's all a class thing."

all previous sales records. A feature film was in the works, with John and Paul working on a dozen new songs for the soundtrack. And there was a booming trade in Beatles paraphernalia: One London factory alone was producing thousands of Beatle wigs a week, and there was a similar mania for collarless jackets and Cuban boots like the ones they favored, plastic "Beatle guitars," and countless other Beatle items.

But they had yet to make a dent in the biggest market of them all. And so they set themselves a new goal: conquering America.

Chapter

5 Invading America

They've got everything over there. What do they want us for?

> —Paul McCartney, en route to America for the first time

So this is America. They all seem out of their minds.

> —Ringo Starr, on his arrival in New York

America, the biggest record market in the world, was the obvious next target for Epstein and "the boys." Anyone who wanted to succeed in the entertainment world had to make it there.

But it was an intimidating prospect, and when they planned their trip there, the Beatles had reason to think it might fail. They knew that no British act had ever made a dent in the American pop charts. They worried that no one would bother listening to a British band. And they knew that efforts to release their records in America had failed. Capitol Records, an American label owned by EMI, had been uninterested in the group even after the group's British successes. The president of Capitol had told Martin flatly, "We don't think the Beatles will do anything in this market."[33]

In desperation, Martin and Epstein had licensed the first Beatles single,

"Please Please Me," to a tiny American label, Vee-Jay. Because of the company's limited distribution and promotion, the record vanished without a trace on the charts. The same thing happened with the second and third American releases, "From Me to You" and "Love Me Do," which Capitol again turned down and which again went to small labels.

But Epstein was not willing to give up. In November 1963, just after the band's appearance before the royal family, the manager flew to New York City to talk to Capitol executives. Although the executives were unenthusiastic, they could not ignore the growing phenomenon of British Beatlemania, and they agreed to release "I Want to Hold Your Hand" in mid-January of the new year.

Epstein also contacted a promoter who wanted to book the Beatles into New York's Carnegie Hall in February. Most important of all, he snagged the engagement that would make the Beatles a household word in America. *The Ed Sullivan Show* had for years been the top TV variety program in America. Variety shows were the most important avenue for acts who wanted national exposure, and they had turned dozens of regional hits like Elvis Presley into national celebrities. Sullivan had witnessed the Beatles phenomenon firsthand while vacationing in England, and he signed them up for two appearances in February.

Down and Up in Paris

Before taking the band to America, Epstein booked them for three weeks in January at Paris's famed Olympia Theater. It was one of the few failures of their careers. For starters, Epstein had agreed to an extremely low fee. He rationalized the poor money by saying that the publicity generated by their appearance at the famous venue would make up for it.

But the shows were disasters. Only a handful of reporters and fans greeted them at the airport. The Beatles were last on a long bill; on opening night it was after midnight when they took the stage and only a few die-hard fans remained. Paul and John made no attempt to speak French or otherwise endear themselves to the audience. The amps kept breaking down. As a final insult, the audience that did stay wanted to hear familiar rock 'n' roll standards and booed the band's originals.

It was their worst gig since the very early days, before they learned to "make show" in front of the rowdy Hamburg crowds. The next day, the Parisian newspapers tore the band's performance to shreds and called them delinquents and has-beens. The remaining shows were nearly as bad. Then came the good news.

It was stunning information, completely unexpected. According to photographer Dezo Hoffman, who had accompanied the band from London, "The Beatles couldn't even speak—not even John Lennon. They just sat on the floor like kittens at Brian's feet."[34] "I Want to Hold Your Hand" was number one in America. And this was a record that was not even supposed to be out in the States!

The reason for the amazing news was a fluke. Back in December, a disc jockey in Washington, D.C., had been given a copy

---

"Nobody Wanted to Know"

In Lennon Remembers, *John describes the almost religious fervor with which the band first brought their music to America.*

"The message was, listen to this music. It was the same in Liverpool—we felt very exclusive and underground in Liverpool listening to all those old time [rock and R&B] records. And nobody was listening to any of them except Eric Burdon in Newcastle and Mick Jagger in London. It was that lonely. It was fantastic. We came over here and it was the same: nobody was listening to rock and roll or to black music in America. We were coming to the land of its origin but nobody wanted to know about it."

George and Paul onstage at the Olympia Theater in Paris. The run at the Olympia in 1964 was a disaster; the Beatles would not attain the instantaneous popularity in France that they would in the United States.

of the British release of "I Want to Hold Your Hand" by his girlfriend, a stewardess with British Overseas Airways. When he played it on the air, the response was so overwhelming that radio stations across the country heard about it and began asking for it. Capitol was suddenly buried in requests for the single.

The release date was bumped up to December 26. A last-minute publicity campaign was hastily devised, including 5 million posters and bumper stickers reading "The Beatles Are Coming!" Disc jockeys were flooded with promotional material, and Capitol distributed quantities of Beatle wigs to its staff across the country. An official memo read:

> As soon as they arrive and until further notice, you and each of your sales and promotion staff are to wear the wig during the business day! . . . Then

offer some to jocks [disc jockeys] and stores for promotions. Get these Beatle wigs around properly, and you'll find you're helping to start the Beatle Hair-Do Craze that should be sweeping the country soon.[35]

The promotion worked. By the time the Beatles heard the news in Paris, American sales had hit 1.5 million. By the time the Beatles arrived in America the following month, full-scale Beatle madness had gripped the nation.

"It's Seven-Thirty, Beatle Time!"

American Beatlemania was created by a number of things. In part it was the sheer quality of the band's musicianship and

Beatle wigs promote the band's arrival in the United States.

personal charm, in part Capitol's promotional efforts, and in part another fluke of timing. A coincidence of timing had catapulted them into England's national consciousness, when their arrival on the national scene cheered up a country frazzled by scandal. Now a similar thing happened in a nation rocked by murder. The assassination of President John F. Kennedy in November 1963 shook America to its core. Through the winter, the United States had been wrapped in shock, grief, and disbelief; Americans were ready for some light news.

When the Beatles and their associates flew to America, however, they had no idea what to expect. They knew that their record was doing well, but everyone was tense and subdued. Neil and the bodyguard Mal spent the flight forging the band's signatures on photographs; the others in the Beatles entourage dozed, played cards, read, and speculated nervously on what was to come. Was the

record a fluke? Would their reception be as hostile as it had been in France?

They need not have worried. When they landed at Kennedy airport in New York on February 7, the Beatles were greeted by five thousand screaming fans. At first the band refused to believe that such a large crowd could be for them; they thought that the president or someone equally important was there at the same time. But the chaotic crowd was for them.

The uproar over the Beatles rivaled anything P. T. Barnum had created for Jenny Lind or that Colonel Tom Parker had drummed up for Elvis Presley. Some newspapers reported later that high school girls had been bribed by promises of free T-shirts to go to the airport and scream for the Beatles—a story that Brian Epstein hotly denied. Bribed or not, the thousands of fans were there—hanging off balconies, straining against a hundred-man police line, screaming their lungs out.

Press photographers were lifted high above the crowds on hydraulic cranes, and two hundred journalists jockeyed for position at a massive press conference. The musicians joked with them as they had done in England: "Are you going to have a haircut while you're in America?" one reporter asked. "We had one yesterday," John replied. "Will you sing something for us?" Again John: "We need money first." "What's your secret?" "If we knew that," George said, "we'd each form a group and manage it."[36]

Eventually the band escaped to the luxurious Plaza Hotel, where their party occupied an entire floor. The reservations had been made months before, when

names like Mr. Lennon or Mr. Starr meant nothing to Americans. When hotel authorities discovered the truth, they worried that riots might destroy their hotel. They tried, unsuccessfully, to convince other hotels to take the band in. In the end, the Plaza staff dealt with the nonstop barrage of girls and reporters as best they could; on several occasions, waiters had to ask patrons in the hotel's posh restaurant to remove their Beatle wigs.

The Beatles were hardly strangers to obsessive attention and howling crowds, but the scale of this American welcome was so much greater than anything they had experienced. The boys were thrilled. They sat in their hotel rooms for hours

The Beatles arrive in New York City in 1964 greeted by thousands of fans. This was only the start of what would be deemed "Beatlemania."

"We Need Money First"

The answers to their first questions with the American press, reprinted in Philip Norman's book Shout!, *show the Beatles at their irreverent best.*

"'Was your family in show business?' John was asked.
'Well, me Dad used to say me Mother was a great performer.'
'Are you part of a teenage rebellion against the older generation?'
'It's a dirty lie.'
'What do you think of the campaign in Detroit to stamp out the Beatles?'
'We've got a campaign of our own,' Paul said, 'to stamp out Detroit.'"

And this excerpt from a San Francisco press conference in 1964, reprinted in The Lost Beatles Interviews, *revolves around a mock campaign to draft Ringo for U.S. president:*

"QUESTION: How about you other guys, how do you feel about Ringo being nominated for president?
JOHN: We think he should win. Definitely in favor.
GEORGE: Yes.
QUESTION: Would you make them part of your cabinet?
RINGO: I'd have to, wouldn't I?
GEORGE: I could be the door.
RINGO: I'd have George as treasurer.
JOHN: I could be the cupboard.
RINGO: George looks after the money."

with their ears glued to transistor radios and their eyes riveted on TV sets, hearing and seeing themselves on every station they switched to.

Most of these stations loved the band and the hoopla. WMCA, a New York pop station, had been playing Beatles music and interviews for weeks, climaxing in a minute-by-minute countdown as the band was en route by plane to New York. The WMCA jockeys gleefully made announcements like, "It's seven-thirty, Beatle time!" Other commentators disdained the Beatles uproar. Chet Huntley of NBC-TV news, for instance, commented on air that he didn't think the band's arrival was an event worth covering, and a disc jockey on WNEW in New York remarked on air that "I Want to Hold Your Hand" made him want to hold his nose.

The *Sullivan Show* and Onward

The day before the band appeared on *The Ed Sullivan Show*, they walked through Central Park accompanied by an estimated four hundred girls and journalists. That evening, most of the band sampled the pleasures of New York's night life, although George went to bed early with a sore throat. Paul visited the Playboy Club and left with one of the club's bunny hostesses. John, Cyn, and Ringo visited another club, the Peppermint Lounge, and Ringo continued on by himself. He returned early the next morning to find the Beatles' staff in a frenzy, fearing he had been kidnapped.

On February 9, Neil Aspinall stood in for a still-ailing George during a rehearsal in Sullivan's studio on West 53rd Street. That evening, some seven hundred lucky fans were in the studio, chosen from over fifty thousand applicants. When they began screaming at the beginning of the show, Sullivan told them to stay quiet until their idols came onstage, warning that the band would not appear unless the crowd could control itself.

After a congratulatory telegram was read from none other than Elvis Presley—the singer who had inspired the Beatles in the first place—the band finally arrived. They performed three songs: "This Boy," "All My Loving," and "She Loves You." For the audience at home, subtitles identified each Beatle by name. John's subtitle also read, "Sorry girls— he's married." Sixty percent of American TV viewers—an estimated 70 million people—witnessed the show; it was the largest audience in the history of television for an entertainment show.

Because of a snowstorm, the Beatles traveled to their next stop, Washington, D.C., by train. Along for the ride were dozens of journalists, several TV crews, and Murray the K, a pushy New York DJ who had "adopted" the Beatles and was calling himself "the Fifth Beatle" because of his supposedly close ties to the band. Three thousand fans were waiting at Union Station for the Beatles, and seven thousand heard them at the Coliseum. Such numbers are common today, but in 1964 an audience of seven thousand was enormous for a pop-culture event.

Ed Sullivan introduces the Beatles. Their performance on The Ed Sullivan Show *was watched by an estimated 70 million people—a number that remains the largest audience in the history of television for an entertainment show.*

Washington, Miami, New York

The fans in Washington had heard about the British habit of throwing candies called jelly babies at the Beatles, which had started when George remarked to a reporter that he liked them. The U.S. fans used jelly beans, the hard-shelled American version of the candy. Ringo later commented that being pelted with solid candies was no fun, but this was offset by the energy level of his first American concert audience. "They hurt like hailstones but they could have ripped me apart and I couldn't have cared less. What an audience! I could have played for them all night!"[37]

Less pleasant was a reception held in the band's honor at the British embassy, where the musicians were exhibited like freaks before the politicians and diplomats. Various officials and their spouses lined up to greet them but acted as if the Beatles were too stupid to understand what was going on. The diplomats lined up for autographs but made cruel comments like, "Do you suppose they can write?" When one woman produced scissors and snipped at Ringo's hair, he and the other Beatles were shocked and outraged. They threatened to start a ruckus, but Brian Epstein got them safely away and promised that nothing so insulting would happen again.

They next returned to New York for their long-sold-out Carnegie Hall shows, where the band was completely drowned out by thousands of screaming fans—among them Happy Rockefeller, wife of New York's governor, and two of her children. Then it was on to Miami, where the band met boxer Cassius Clay, who would soon change his name to Muhammad Ali. The flamboyant boxer lifted Ringo in the air and announced to reporters that the Beatles were the greatest—but that he was

The Beatles relax during a short yacht cruise while in Miami in 1964.

From Pompadours to Bangs

Writer Patrick Snyder, in a 1973 article in Crawdaddy *magazine reprinted in* The Beatles Reader, *comments on the band's immediate impact on America.*

"In the negative, disoriented reality of America in January, 1964, the Beatles became a safety valve for the release of trauma-wrought tensions. They replaced a ruptured American dream with a new dream that valued love, and holding hands, and dancing with you above all else. Peter, Paul and Mary, The Kingston Trio and the Brothers Four, with their songs of gentle protest and bittersweet romance, simply disappeared from the singles market; their lilting melodies and literary lyrics could simply not match the nimble energy of the Beatles.

By the time February rolled around, Beatlemania had seized the nation and 75% of its television sets tuned in to Ed Sullivan to get a glimpse of the four young men responsible for all this furor. Out they came, John ('Sorry girls, he's married'), Paul, George and Ringo, and unlike the previous decade's pop idols, they didn't seem the least bit dangerous or licentious. In fact, they were cute with their happy grins and spiffy suits that seemed a bit too small. Of course, their hair was totally outrageous and carefully lubricated pompadours all over America became fluffy bangs overnight.

For months afterward, the Beatles were responsible for centuries of after-school detention as they fueled endless panting discussions in study halls and classrooms all over America. The insides of locker doors were plastered with their pictures and radios and record players (what's a stereo?) blasted their music almost constantly. Amidst the Beatle hours, the Beatle days, and even the Beatle weeks (very difficult with less than two dozen songs), you would tune in each Friday to find out if your favorite was number one this time around. Singlehandedly, they accounted for 60% of the retail record sales in the top hundred, including positions one through five."

still the prettiest. On February 16, 75 million people watched the band's second appearance on *The Ed Sullivan Show*, broadcast live from the ballroom of the Hotel Deauville.

In Miami they had time to shop for records, watch an Elvis movie at a drive-in, and relax by the ocean. Taken for a cruise in a record company executive's yacht, Ringo asked to steer the ship and nearly ran it aground. As he later recalled, no one seemed to mind very much; he was mortified, but the Americans were just thrilled to be in the presence of the Beatles.

Reactions in America to the Beatles invasion were mixed. The *New York Herald Tribune* sniffed that they were "75% public-ity, 20% haircut and 5% lilting lament." The *Washington Post* called them "asexual and homely."[38] Religious leaders and other authorities around the country, meanwhile, spoke out angrily about the decline in morality created by Beatlemania.

But the public's response is what counted, and in that area the band's American venture was a triumph. Their concerts were record-breaking sensations. *Newsweek* honored them with a cover story. Sales of records and merchandise rocketed. There were even dozens of tribute records—songs with titles like "We Love You Beatles," "My Boyfriend Got a Beatle Haircut," and "Ringo for President." The Beatles, against all odds, had conquered the States.

6 The Beatlemania Years

It was a brotherhood. It was like a fort, really, with four corners, that was impregnable.
—George Martin

They are my brothers, you see. I'm an only child, and they're my brothers.
—Ringo Starr

When I feel my head start to swell, I look at Ringo and know perfectly well we're not supermen.
—John Lennon

Throughout 1964 and '65, Beatlemania spread like wildfire on both sides of the Atlantic. Everyone—rich, poor, young, old, and in-between—seemed to be talking about the Beatles, buying Beatles music, following the Beatles' every move. Their songs were on the air all the time, each new release outdoing the last in sales and popularity. As Epstein's business associate Peter Brown once put it, "It seemed as if nothing else was being played on the radio."[39]

One measure of their popularity was the number of successful British groups they inspired. These bands, known as the British Invasion after they successfully stormed the American charts, included the Hollies, the Animals, the Who, the Dave Clark Five, and the Rolling Stones. The members of these bands, many of them friends of the Beatles, shared an en-

thusiasm for American blues, rock, and R&B. They would often get together to talk about music, listen to records, and swap songs.

Another measure of popularity was the number of official honors the Beatles received. The Variety Club of Great Britain named them "Show Business Personality of the Year" for 1964. Madame Tussaud's Wax Museum, a famous London landmark, exhibited life-size models of the band. Even the venerable *Encyclopaedia Britannica* gave the group its own entry.

The most visible honor came when British prime minister Harold Wilson announced in June 1965 that the Beatles would receive one of England's most prestigious awards, the MBE (Member of the British Empire). In large part this honor was made because of the impact Beatlemania had on the British economy, generating enormous amounts of money. Many Britons were outraged that a group of scruffy longhairs could receive such a prestigious honor; several holders of the award returned theirs in protest.

The Beatles were typically offhand about the affair. Ringo said he'd keep his medal to dust when he got old, and George said wryly, "I didn't think you got that sort of thing just for playing rock and

The Beatles hold out their MBE awards for a 1965 publicity photo. The MBE is considered one of England's most prestigious awards.

roll music."[40] After a ceremony in which Queen Elizabeth presented the band with their medals, Paul told reporters that the queen was a very nice person, like someone's mother. John Lennon claimed later that the band smoked marijuana in a Buckingham Palace bathroom just before the ceremony, although the other Beatles have since stated that the only things smoked that day, out of nervousness, were ordinary cigarettes.

Image Versus Reality

Part of Epstein's job was to make sure that stories like the one about smoking grass in Buckingham Palace were kept secret. He made sure that the band's image main-

tained its mixture of irreverence and cleanliness. He instructed "the boys" to be silent on how they hated their travel schedules and their robotlike performances night after night. He made sure that no mention was made of the constant stream of girls in and out of the Beatles' hotel suites. Nor did the public ever discover how cruel the band could be toward someone they didn't like.

As time went on, it became increasingly difficult for the band to hide its dirty laundry. For one thing, the band was plagued by a series of paternity suits, in which women claimed members of the band were the fathers of their children. Two such cases against Paul were settled out of court before the band became famous. By the time the Beatles became a household word, however, all of them were deluged with similar claims. Most were proven false, but even so the suits were time-consuming, expensive, and damaging. Such potential scandals became increasingly commonplace as the band continued its manic race through the Beatlemania years.

The press was only too happy to maintain the band's public persona: the lovable mop tops, the Fab Four, a bunch of Liverpool boys who didn't take themselves seriously but who knew how to deliver one-liners and great pop tunes with honesty and charm. There was little effort

A Loving Rivalry

Producer George Martin was in a better position than almost anyone else to observe the intense love and strong rivalry between John Lennon and Paul McCartney, as well as the way in which George Harrison's songwriting efforts were kept in check. This excerpt is from his book With a Little Help from My Friends.

"John Lennon and Paul McCartney in particular were extremely good friends; they loved one another, really. They shared a spirit of adventure, and a modest little childhood ambition: they were going to go out and conquer the world. You could, though, almost touch the rivalry between them, it was so intense and so real, despite this overriding warmth. No sooner would John come up with an outstanding song evoking, say, his own early childhood, like 'Strawberry Fields Forever,' than Paul answered him straight back with a winner in the same vein: 'Penny Lane.'

It was typical of the way they worked as a song-writing duo. Creative rivalry kept them climbing their individual ladders—and kept the Beatles on top. John would write 'In My Life,' and go up a rung; Paul would go one rung higher still with 'Yesterday.' Often they would help each other out on a song, if they were stuck—despite their dual composer credits. For the most part, though, they egged each other on by the brilliant example of their individual efforts. . . .

The electricity that crackled between Paul and John, and that led to such great music, rather left George out in the cold. He had only himself to collaborate with. If he needed help from the other two, they gave it, but often rather grudgingly. It was not so much that Lennon and McCartney did not believe in Harrison; more that their overwhelming belief in themselves left very little room for anything—or anybody—else."

then, unlike today, to reveal nasty secrets or unpleasant details.

One example of this came in April 1964, when John Lennon published *In His Own Write*, a book of poems, stories, and cartoons. Critics loved the book's wit, strangeness, and originality, and they compared Lennon favorably to famous writers like Lewis Carroll and James Joyce. *In His Own Write* received a prestigious literary prize, the Foyle Award. At a lavish luncheon in his honor, Lennon was asked to make a short speech. According to Peter Brown, the author was so hungover that all he could do was stand up and mumble, "Thank you very much."

This was somehow interpreted by reporters as "You've got a lucky face." They dutifully noted that this strange comment was another example of Lennon's brilliance. Brown, however, saw the incident as simply another example of the press's unquestioning adulation of a band that could do no wrong: "Once again," he noted, "the king wore no clothes but never caught cold."[41]

They're Gonna Put Me in the Movies

Both *In His Own Write* and its successor, *A Spaniard in the Works*, sold well. A much greater impact was made on the world, however, by two feature movies starring the Beatles.

Their film debut, *A Hard Day's Night*, was a milestone in the marriage of popular music and movies. It directly influenced virtually all later rock movies as well as MTV-style videos. Referring to director-star Orson Welles's first movie, which

many people consider the greatest movie ever made, one critic called *A Hard Day's Night* at the time of its release "the *Citizen Kane* of juke-box musicals."

Previous rock 'n' roll movies had been cheap, quickly made exploitation films with meager plots, awful dialogue, and worse acting. But for *A Hard Day's Night*, playwright Alun Owen, a Liverpudlian brought in at the Beatles' request, wrote a funny, inventive script about a typical day in the life of the band. Much of Owen's witty dialogue was lifted directly from conversations he overheard while traveling with the group. (The title came from a phrase Ringo once used to describe the band's exhausting schedule.)

The film was shot in just six weeks with a tiny budget, most of which was spent simply avoiding crowds. Besides Owen and the Beatles, the movie's key people were two Americans living in London, producer Walter Shenson and director Richard Lester. Lester had the Beatles' approval because he had directed a short film starring their beloved Goons. His manic, slapstick, surrealistic style was a perfect match with the Beatles' own subversive humor.

The film firmly established in the minds of Beatles fans the public personalities of the band: John was witty and cheeky; Paul, kind and cute; George, shy; Ringo, homely and lovable. All four proved to be natural actors, evoking comparisons with the Marx Brothers. Ringo in particular was excellent, especially in a touching, bittersweet scene where he wandered forlornly beside a canal. Ringo later admitted that he was so hungover on the day of the shoot that he didn't have to pretend being slow and miserable.

Over a hundred thousand fans lined the streets to greet the Beatles at the

The Beatles on the set of A Hard Day's Night. *In the book* Lennon Remembers, *John claimed the band was dissatisfied with the film's writing: "We were a bit infuriated by the glibness of it and the . . . dialogue."*

movie's premiere in July 1964, and the audience included two royal admirers, Princess Margaret and Lord Snowdon. Both the film and its soundtrack were immensely popular. The soundtrack, one of the best of all the Beatles records, has one curious aspect: It is the only Beatles album ever to contain nothing but Lennon-McCartney songs, with no songs by other writers.

The First World Tour

Early in June, the band began a massive tour of Europe, the Far East, Australia, and America. No other rock 'n' roll entertainers had ever made such a large or lengthy undertaking and as they went, the Beatles virtually invented the now-familiar concept of the rock tour.

Ringo missed part of it because he had his tonsils removed and another drummer, Jimmy Nichol, took his place. In interviews, Nichol said he was delighted to be a temporary Beatle and hoped it would be a career boost for him, although he faded into obscurity after Ringo rejoined the band in Australia in mid-June.

This first world tour was a roaring success, with screaming crowds and sold-out auditoriums everywhere. To the musicians, however, it was as much a blur as any of their previous jaunts. They conquered the world but saw little of it—just a jumble of hotels, limousines, stages, and planes.

Everywhere they went the Beatles also encountered dull questions from reporters and offensive behavior from strangers, which they fought with humor. In Australia John's Aunt Mimi, who was

"A Long, High-Pitched Wailing Sound"

In this excerpt from his book The Love You Make, *Beatles business associate Peter Brown reflects on Beatlemania at its manic peak.*

"If you had to characterize the Beatles' first [full] tour of America, it would be a sound, a long, high-pitched wailing sound that assailed their ears from the time their plane touched ground in San Francisco on August 18 to the moment they left America four weeks later. It was the screams of hysterical girls at the airport and the whining of their rented Lockheed Electra; it was the wail of the police sirens and motorcycles that escorted them and the shrieking of girls waiting in hallways and the streets. Hoping to see a bit of America, all they got to see were the back seats of limousines, antiseptic hotel suites, institutionalized meals from room service shared with aggressive journalists or loudmouthed disc jockeys, dank dressing rooms in the lockers of athletic stadiums. . . .

At their opening night concert at the Cow Palace in San Francisco, their limousine driver didn't pull away from the stadium loading ramp quickly enough and the Beatles' car was overrun by hysterical teenagers. The weight of the people began to crush the roof, with the Beatles inside. Only the quick action of the Cow Palace security forces extricated the boys in time. . . .

On August 20 they performed at Convention Hall in Las Vegas, and on the twenty-first they were at Municipal Stadium in Seattle, where a girl climbed high over the stage on a beam to get a closer look at them and fell in a heap at Ringo's feet. On the twenty-second they were at the Empire Stadium in Vancouver, Canada, and on August 23 there was a triumphant concert at the Hollywood Bowl, where the towels they used to wipe their bodies after the concert were cut up into square inch souvenirs and mounted on certificates for sale. The twenty-sixth found them in Denver at the Red Rock Stadium, the twenty-seventh at the Gardens in Cincinnati, where Brian disappeared. . . . Ringo went on a binge of amphetamines and liquor in Indianapolis, showed up just in time for show and could barely play."

accompanying them, told a television talk-show host that John had been bad at math. The reporter asked John how he counted all his money and John replied, "I don't count it—I weigh it."[42] On another occasion a woman rudely asked Lennon for an autograph; she then turned to a friend and said, "I never thought I would stoop to asking for such an autograph." John replied, "And I never thought that I would be forced to sign my name for someone like you."[43]

Things were no less strange and exhausting on the American leg of their tour: twenty-three cities in about six weeks, with an average of six hundred miles of travel a day. Beatlemania was in full flower all through the tour. The band was sometimes conveyed through crowds in special iron cages. Entrepreneurs everywhere sold items like "canned Beatle breath." Bed linens and towels used by the band were bought at every stop, cut into small squares, and resold at huge profits. The craziness reached a peak when the Beatles returned to *The Ed Sullivan Show* and then on August 15 appeared at New York's Shea Stadium before fifty-six thousand fans, the largest crowd ever assembled for a show. The tour ended in late September with a final performance in San Francisco.

A young woman tries to break through a police barricade to touch the stage where the Beatles had performed the night before. This scene would be repeated many times and in many different ways once Beatlemania took hold of Americans.

"Like Lemmings"

In his official biography, The Beatles, *Hunter Davies describes Beatlemania at its peak.*

"There was perpetual screaming and yeh-yehing for three years, one long continuous succession of hysterical teenagers of every class and color, shouting uncontrollably, not one of whom could hear what was going on for the noise of each other. Each of them emotionally, mentally, or sexually excited, foaming at the mouth, bursting into tears, hurling themselves like lemmings in the direction of the Beatles or just simply fainting.

Throughout the whole of the three years it was happening somewhere in the world. Each country witnessed the same scenes of mass emotion, scenes which had never been thought possible before and which are unlikely to be ever seen again. Writing about it now makes it all sound like fiction. It is impossible to exaggerate Beatlemania because Beatlemania was in itself an exaggeration. No words can fully describe those scenes, although every major newspaper in the world has miles of words and pictures in its clipping library, giving blow-by-blow accounts of what happened when the Beatles descended on their part of the globe. Once it had stopped, by 1967, and everyone was either overcome by exhaustion or boredom, it was difficult to believe it had all happened. Could everyone have been so mad? It wasn't just teenagers; people of all ages and all intellects had succumbed, though perhaps not all as hysterically as the teenagers."

Fans at the Los Angeles airport react hysterically as the Beatles' plane makes a brief stopover.

There was one tragedy. While the band was staying at San Francisco's Hilton Hotel a woman was shot and killed, but her body was not discovered for several hours because her screams, heard by chambermaids, were thought to have been made by Beatles fans. The incident made the Beatles, already mindful of the still-recent assassination of President Kennedy, even more worried than before about their own safety.

Expanding the Recordings

The adulation, money, and record-breaking attendances were exciting, but the long tour took a serious toll on the band. By the end of 1964, the Beatles were drained physically, emotionally, and artistically. The band's next album, released just before Christmas, reflected this exhaustion. Even its British title, *Beatles for Sale*, hinted at despair.

As composers, Lennon and McCartney were at a low ebb. (George Harrison had been writing songs for several years, but none of them had been chosen yet for recording.) As a result, *Beatles for Sale* has more cover versions than any other Beatles album. Even the originals are weak. One example is "I'll Follow the Sun," written by Paul when he was sixteen. He had always thought the song was not good enough to record, but by 1965 he was desperate enough to use it.

Although many critics and fans feel *Beatles for Sale* is the poorest album the band ever made, it was still light-years ahead of anything other pop groups were producing. Even their chief rivals for chart dominance, bands like the Rolling Stones and the Beach Boys, could not match it. And despite its overall poor quality, the album has some fine touches, especially in Martin's production; for example, the guitar feedback on "I Feel Fine" may be the first recorded version of deliberate distortion, and "Eight Days a Week" was probably the first song ever to have a fade-in rather than the more conventional fade-out.

In America, *Beatles for Sale* was released as *Beatles '65*. Not just the title was different. Until the release of *Sgt. Pepper*, American and British versions of Beatles albums differed both in the number of songs and in their order. Capitol Records, the American label, routinely eliminated one or two tracks from each British version and withheld them, saving them to create "new" albums. Later CD reissues retain the original British versions.

Fortunately, the group's artistic slump was temporary, and their next recordings returned to a high level of excellence. Much of the credit for this belongs to Martin, who continued to believe in the Beatles, never cheating or selling them out and remaining content to do what he did best—edit, arrange, and polish their raw material.

Martin constantly pushed the band to improve their material and to experiment with new recording techniques. This experimentation began with a few touches on *Beatles for Sale* and became even bolder with their next recordings. Studio Two at Abbey Road, by now virtually the Beatles' exclusive studio, converted to four-track technology. This opened up new worlds for Martin and the band; no longer did they have to make recordings that were essentially just re-creations of their live shows.

A scene from Help! *Although the movie suffered from a somewhat dull plot, its title track remains one of the most popular Beatles songs.*

By early 1965, the Beatles were back in the studio to record a set of songs for their second film, *Help!* Among these was one that would become the most famous Beatles song of all: "Yesterday," a melody that came to Paul McCartney in a dream.

Help!, originally entitled *Eight Arms to Hold You*, was filmed in the spring and released that summer. It was directed by Richard Lester with a large budget that allowed shooting in color on location around the world. Though it was another smash hit, *Help!* is less inspired than the band's first movie. It is saddled with a silly and vaguely racist script about a group of Indian religious fanatics trying to retrieve a sacred ring that Ringo has innocently acquired. The movie also falls down in showcasing the personalities of the band; the musicians later commented that they felt as if they were walking in on someone else's film.

But by then they were on to other things. By midsummer, the Beatles were heavily into their experimentation with both song structure and studio techniques—and they were not the only ones. The summer of 1965 was a time of major change in pop music around the world. The Beatles rose to the challenge, and the next period of their career was both a creative high point and the end of their public performances.

Chapter

7 Controversy and Change

What we really wanted was to turn you on to the truth rather than just bloody pot!

—Paul McCartney

The Beatles' strange new lives gave them many chances to experiment—with music, with lifestyles, with the ability to do whatever they chose. They had money, which they used with pleasure; and they used their fame to speak out with increasing candor on issues. But they also discovered that money and fame isolated them from the everyday world, and that the power celebrity brought was not always positive. Soon, the pressures of being Beatles would send them down different, and often controversial, new paths.

Brian Epstein found a financial adviser for his rich young clients, who advised buying houses. John, George, and Ringo each bought a plush home in the suburbs of London; Paul opted for one in St. John's Wood, only a short distance from the Abbey Road studios. Each Beatle also bought a home for his parents (in John's case, his Aunt Mimi). Paul bought his father a racehorse, John bought three cars although he had never learned to drive, and Ringo spent a small fortune on camera equipment and soon was a skilled photographer.

The Beatles' romantic lives were gradually becoming more settled. Paul's long-

time girlfriend Jane Asher more or less moved into the house in St. John's Wood. Ringo married his Liverpool sweetheart, hairdresser Maureen Cox, and in September 1965 they had their first child. In early 1966 George married Pattie Boyd, a model he had met when she was an extra on *A Hard Day's Night.* John did his best to

John and George with their wives. While John had been married to Cynthia before his Beatle fame, George married model Pattie Boyd in 1966.

be a good family man, though he was increasingly restless and bored with his home life.

Their instant recognizability was increasingly cutting them off from the world. Avoiding crowds was virtually a full-time job. Any precious time off was spent on vacation in far-off places where they would not be recognized. When the Beatles ate out, they chose extremely fancy restaurants where they would not be bothered. As Ringo put it in an interview, in such places "the people are such drags, such snobs, you see, that they won't bother to come over to your table. They pretend they don't even know who you are, and you get away with an easy night."[44]

They also began experimenting with drugs besides liquor. According to several sources, their friend Bob Dylan introduced them to marijuana. By the spring of 1965 it had replaced alcohol as their drug of choice, and all of them were regularly smoking grass by the time *Help!* was filmed.

Rubber Soul and *Revolver*

The summer of 1965, musically speaking, can be broadly summarized as the time when rock 'n' roll became rock. Everywhere, pop musicians were experimenting with new forms. The music expanded widely from its roots in R&B and blues, merging with folk and other musical strains to create a vast array of different styles. Eventually these would be known by names like folk rock and acid rock.

Another change was an increasing emphasis on the lyrics of songs. For years, even the best songwriters (Lennon and McCartney included) had paid little attention to what their songs said. Now, for the first time in years, the words of pop songs were as important as the music. They had serious meaning and real content.

The best of the current songwriters began to take themselves as seriously as any poet, addressing social and political issues such as civil rights and war. Typical were some of that summer's big hits: "Mr. Tambourine Man," a Bob Dylan song that the Byrds transformed into a ringing rock anthem; the Rolling Stones' "Satisfaction," with its nasty guitar riff and bold, sexy lyrics; and Dylan's own epic "Like a Rolling Stone."

For the Beatles, these songs were serious calls to action; they made it clear that it wasn't enough anymore to be simply a group of lovable mop tops. Away from the special and unique atmosphere of Beatlemania, rock writer Geoffrey Stokes has noted, "pop music was in the process of becoming a little more than fun."[45]

The next Beatles album, *Rubber Soul*, recorded in the fall of 1965 and released in December, vigorously answered the challenge. Songs like "Norwegian Wood," "In My Life," and "Think for Yourself" clearly showed McCartney, Lennon, and Harrison (who was finally getting some of his songs on albums) paying close attention to literary and artistic expression. For the first time, the band was creating music for listening as well as dancing.

The album after *Rubber Soul* took them even further. Instead of the clean, polished sound the Beatles had always created, the songs on *Revolver* featured feedback, tape loops, electronically altered voices, and other wild effects. Such techniques have since become standard in pop music, but they were revolutionary at the time.

"Dragging Around the World"

"One of the reasons given was that their music had developed so much, using full orchestras and electronic devices, that they couldn't possibly perform it onstage any more.

This is true to a great extent. But the real reason was that for a long, long time they had hated what they were doing. They disliked dragging around the world, appearing publicly in a glass box like a peep show. They disliked performing onstage in the same old way. They thought it was a farce, a mockery. Neil and Mal, their road managers, disliked the tensions, the panic and the chaos of it all.

'Open-air concerts in the States were terrible,' says Mal. 'We were in this baseball field once. There they were, stuck out on their own in the middle of the field with 30,000 kids screaming and waiting to hear them. I said to the promoter, where's the outlet, chief? He said, "What? They play guitars, don't they?" He hadn't realized they used electric guitars. We had a right panic getting electricians to lay on wires in time.' . . .

'We learned always to go on at the very last minute, if not later,' says Neil. 'If we went too early they just got mobbed on the way from the dressing room. But if they had to run like mad after they were supposed to be on, people would get out of the way and let them through. We did this with our first Ed Sullivan show in New York. He was sweating like a pig, convinced we were going to be late. It was a live show as well. He blamed me for it all, for just doing it.' . . .

'No one eventually enjoyed touring. You can't really. Once you've got to manufacture it, it doesn't work. You've got to give to receive. Some nights we'd feel it had been terrible. We didn't give anything. That was when we decided we should give it up, before others started disliking it as well.'"

Revolver also featured the broadest set of songwriting styles the band had ever used. The songs ranged from a straightforward rocker like "Taxman" and an elegantly simple love song like "Here, There, and Everywhere" to the moody strings of "Eleanor Rigby," the goofy underwater sounds of "Yellow Submarine," the north Indian classical instruments on "Love You To," and the eerie effects of "Tomorrow Never Knows."

The Butcher Cover

Coinciding with the band's second world tour in 1966, Capitol Records released *Yesterday . . . and Today*, an album composed mostly of leftover songs that had not appeared on the American versions of *Rubber Soul* and *Help!* This record has the distinction of being the only Beatles LP ever to lose money for Capitol.

The fault was not poor sales; in fact the record sold very well. The reason was a controversial jacket photo that showed the Beatles dressed in white coats and covered with baby-doll parts and hunks of bloody meat. This so-called butcher cover photo resulted from a last-minute idea during a photo shoot, when the Beatles had been trying out unusual ideas to get away from the dull routine of group photos.

It is unclear how Capitol—much less the always vigilant Brian Epstein—could have allowed the cover's release, since it clearly undermined the band's wholesome image. But it did slip past, and some 750,000 copies were released before a storm of protest from disgusted fans and others caused Capitol to withdraw it. The company quickly pasted an innocuous group photo over some of the butcher covers, and in some cases the offending shot was torn off and replaced altogether. The expense involved in this hasty recall cost Capitol the profit for this album.

Thousands of fans across the United States bought copies of the album and steamed off the "clean" photo in an effort to find the butcher shot underneath. The original cover became an instant collector's item, and a copy in good condition now sells for a small fortune. John Lennon was furious when Capitol recalled the butcher-cover records and used the controversy as an opportunity to speak out, something he was doing more often despite Epstein's efforts to rein him in. Referring to a topic just coming into the public eye, John said the banned cover was "as relevant as Vietnam."[46]

"More Popular than Jesus"

On the Far Eastern leg of their tour, the band accidentally caused another controversy in the Philippines. Imelda Marcos, the wife of dictator Fernando Marcos, had arranged a lavish reception for the band. Unfortunately, the reception was set for the band's day off, and they politely declined to give up their precious private time. Somehow their reply never reached the hostess, and when they failed to arrive for her huge party, she went on live television to protest the insult.

The next day's headlines blared BEATLES SNUB PRESIDENT, and the entire country was ablaze with anger. Epstein went on Filipino television to try and explain the situation, but it did no good. The British embassy received death threats, there were

The Beatles at a press conference after offending Imelda Marcos, wife of dictator Fernando Marcos.

demonstrations in several cities, and promoters refused to pay the band's fees. When the group left the islands, there was no police protection from angry crowds, and customs officials at the airport jeered, punched, and kicked the musicians. The final insult came when an income tax official held up the Beatles' flight until he was paid seven thousand pounds he claimed the Beatles owed.

The butcher cover and the insult to Imelda Marcos were minor, however, compared to the uproar caused that summer by another of John's public statements.

In the spring, London *Evening Standard* reporter Maureen Cleave had published an extensive profile of Lennon. John had always been cynical about organized religion. During the interview, he had expressed sadness that a pop band could become more popular than a reli-gious leader, though he noted that both would fade in time. Cleave quoted him as saying, "Christianity will go. It will vanish and shrink. . . . We're more popular than Jesus now. I don't know which will go first—rock and roll or Christianity."[47] Lennon went on to say that he had nothing against Christ or Christian teachings, but that in his opinion people who tried to twist Christ's words were in the wrong.

The reaction in England was not strong; to Britons, it was apparently just another remark, the kind of thing John often threw out to outrage people. But the reaction in America was different when a teen magazine, *Datebook*, reprinted a portion of the Lennon interview later that year. The story was widely repeated and as it swept across the United States Lennon was often quoted inaccurately or out of context.

"Because They Played Good Music"

Critic Stephen Holroyd, writing in the British newspaper Melody Maker *in 1966 (an article reprinted in* The Beatles Reader*), says that the lasting success of the Beatles is primarily because of their music.*

"The Beatles made it because they played good music. If they had all been bald it would scarcely have made any difference. They have become the most phenomenally successful artists in the history of entertainment because of their music. In fact (protect me from their 273 million teenage fans) they have very little else to offer as entertainers.

Like Frank Sinatra, they are good singers of good songs—and that is why they are world-beaters, not because they make funny quips at press conferences, not because they come from Liverpool, not because they have been skillfully promoted. . . .

What exactly did the Beatles do?

One thing is certain—it's not a bit of good asking them. And this, in a way, is a clue to their success. They did what came naturally and were unfettered [unchained] by the musical conventions which for so long had determined the structure of pop songs.

John Lennon and Paul McCartney have great gifts of melodic invention, a natural ear for harmony and an original concept of song construction which results, in part, from their complete lack of musical training.

Brilliant arrangers and orchestrators with years of training and experience behind them would give their right arms to be able to write songs like 'Michelle' and 'If I Fell.' They just can't do it because they lack that freshness of approach. Their musical minds are corrupted by orthodoxy and commerciality. Sure they can write a nice, slick, glib and polished original—but it will never have that spark which distinguishes a great song from a professionally competent one."

The result was an enormous backlash of anti-Beatle sentiment. Conservative public and religious leaders spoke out bitterly against the group. Dozens of radio stations banned their music, and a number of influential groups urged a boycott of Beatles products. Protests were staged by groups like the Ku Klux Klan. Records by the allegedly godless group were burned in public bonfires across the country. As the controversy spread, the Beatles were banned in South Africa and Spain and condemned by the pope.

The uproar devastated Brian Epstein. Suddenly, the public perception of the Beatles had changed from that of four lovable mop tops to that of some angry, in-your-face band like the Stones, the Who, or the Animals. Epstein flew to America ahead of the band to try to calm the waters, but with little luck; the American press, uninterested in Epstein, was eager to hear what Lennon himself had to say.

When John landed with the rest of the group in America in mid-August, he faced packs of journalists in every city. This time, they were not as friendly as before. Again and again he tried to clarify what he had meant. He had simply used the Beatles as a handy example of mass adulation, he said; he "could have said TV or the cinema, motor cars or anything popular and . . . gotten away with it."[48] Over and over he made comments like,

> I'm sorry I opened my mouth. I'm not anti-God, anti-Christ or anti-religion. I wouldn't knock it. I didn't mean we were greater or better. . . . I apologize, if that will make you [reporters] happy. I still don't know quite what I've done. I've tried to tell you what I did do, but if you want me to apologize, if that will make you happy, then okay, I'm sorry![49]

Christians burn Beatles records to protest John Lennon's remark that the Beatles were more popular than Jesus.

Brian Epstein arrives in New York in 1966 to try to contain the furor created over John Lennon's controversial remark about the Beatles' popularity. The remark was one indicator that the Beatles were tiring of the strict control Epstein had placed on their behavior.

The End of Touring

The controversy over John's remark was indicative of one of the changes happening to the Beatles. More and more, the Beatles were slipping out of Brian Epstein's control. John Lennon in particular was beginning to break away from the restrictions imposed on him. He began venting publicly some of his tremendous rage and anger—anger at himself for not fulfilling his role as an artist, anger at his unsatisfying personal life, anger at injustices he saw in the world. The "more popular than Jesus" controversy was merely the most public example of his penchant for speaking his mind, sometimes foolishly but always passionately.

There were other serious changes taking place. Even before the craziness of Beatlemania had taken hold, the band had begun to dislike touring. By now, they actively hated it.

After a while no amount of money or fame could compensate them for what they endured on tour. They were exhausted all the time and rarely had a chance even to eat properly. They were besieged in their hotels and mobbed when they tried to escape. All the benefits—the money and glamour, the girls and drink and drugs, the occasional pleasant interlude like the evening they spent with their idol, Elvis Presley—could not make up for the fact that their lives had become one big hotel suite.

Perhaps most of all, the Beatles were worried about their music. In the early Liverpool and Hamburg days, they had been challenged to mature and grow musically. Even their early tours had allowed them hour-long sets in which to perfect their skills and songs. But fame changed everything. Now the shows were a half hour long, the sequence of songs identical every night.

Also, they could never listen to themselves. The art of putting on stadium-size concerts was still in its infancy—the Beatles, after all, virtually invented the concept of the rock tour—and their setups were always inadequate. For instance, there were never any monitors, the speakers bands use to hear themselves clearly.

Between the lack of monitors, the overboosted amplifiers, and the always-present screaming crowd, they never heard themselves. They lost the beat and sang off-key. Often they simply mimed the words. The audience didn't seem to care very much; it was enough to be in the presence of the

Mountains out of Molehills

In this section of an article written in the British newspaper the Spectator *in August 1966 and reprinted in* The Beatles Reader, *David Frost comments on how out of proportion the controversy then surrounding John Lennon's "more popular than Jesus" comment was.*

"Even the current explosion may not have been 100 per cent genuine. For the first day or two, the stories coming over the wires from New York were alarmingly general in their first paragraphs—stations were banning Beatle records, organising burning ceremonies, American teenagers were revolting, and so on—but always suspiciously vague when it came to particular examples, which seemed to hinge mainly on one Mr. Tommy Charles of station WAQY in Birmingham, Alabama—scarcely the barometer of the American nation. . . .

[T]he story reached its denouement when the Beatles office in London issued a long and extraordinarily detailed apology and denial [that] concludes: 'In the circumstances John is deeply concerned and regrets that people with deep religious beliefs should have been offended in any way.'

Well . . . what does one make of all that? It is not merely a question of what you think of John Lennon's original statement. You may think it was splendidly refreshing to hear a pop singer speaking his mind, whether you agreed or disagreed with what he was saying. Or you may just have thought that the Beatles were going too far and ought to be stopped by some means or other. That, however, is basically irrelevant.

First and foremost, the [apology] does not really reflect the feelings of John Lennon at the moment he made the original remark. Secondly . . . it does not really reflect the views of the Beatles' fans either here or in New York. . . . Thirdly, of course, the statement does not really reflect the true feelings of our two societies. . . . The Beatles' statement has been wrung out of them by society for their failure to adhere to a code which in the main the Beatles themselves have rejected, their fans have rejected, and that self-same society has rejected."

Beatles. But the band hated it, and they routinely told their opening acts not to listen because they sounded so terrible. Adding to their frustration was the fact that they were in a particularly fertile period of songwriting, as *Rubber Soul* and the just-released *Revolver* showed.

On top of all these problems was the very real threat of violence against the now-controversial band. Death threats were frequent in America. At a concert in Memphis the group plunged into a near panic when they mistook a firecracker for a gunshot. The crowds screaming for attention and jumping on their cars were more terrifying than ever.

By the time the band played its final show of that tour—at San Francisco's Candlestick Park on August 29—they were at the end of their rope. In the air the next day, bound for home, George Harrison uttered a comment, only half-jokingly, that summed up their weariness: "That's it, I'm not a Beatle anymore."[50]

The Beatles appear on The Ed Sullivan Show in 1966. By this time, they had grown weary of touring and performing live.

"The Mayor of Whozis"

Writer Geoffrey Stokes, in his book The Beatles, *has this to say about how the craziness of touring affected the band.*

"After a while . . . the touring made them prisoners. Ostensibly available to their fans, they were in fact sealed off from the world. Their hotels were besieged, their getaway cars mobbed. Despite—or perhaps because of—the interchangeable parade of groupies, their lives became one indistinguishable hotel room, with cabin fever its invariable accompaniment.

But they were trapped by more than circumstances, for the times themselves made them hypocrites. Thinking back on the lovable lads of *A Hard Day's Night*, one has to struggle to remember just who their real-life counterparts were. As John remembers, 'I mean, we had this one image, but man, our tours were like something else . . . the Beatles tours were like [the nightmarish film] Fellini's *Satyricon*.' These were four increasingly mean, amphetamine-gobbling, gonzo drunks. Who had to make nice to everyone.

The Mayor of Whozis wanted his picture taken with Ringo? Swell. Nothing the boys would like better. Radio WWWW wanted a quick interview with John? Of course. No trouble at all. Just wait till we extract the Mayor of Whozis' teenage daughter from his shower, okay? Whozis' polyester DJ version of the Fifth Beatle wanted an exclusive with Paul? Absolutely. Tell him to bring the pills to Room 1633—and this time he should bring a couple of extra girls for the roadies, too. Sorry, no interviews with George. He's too busy throwing up right now."

Shortly after their return to England, the band made a major decision. They would not tour anymore. Instead, they would concentrate on studio recordings.

It was a bold and brave move. No pop musician had ever survived by selling records. Even Elvis Presley made two movies a year during the years he was not performing live. By quitting the road, the Beatles risked losing their huge audience. As writer Hunter Davies has noted, very few entertainers retire at the peak of their popularity. But, Davies wrote, "The Beatles had no hesitation. They saw it as the end of Chapter One."[51]

Chapter

8 The Summer of Love and Death

You wouldn't want to hear the Beatles doing "Mr. Kite" on a [modern] forty-eight-track machine, it wouldn't have the same charm.

—George Harrison

The *anthem of the Sixties counterculture, a perfect articulation of its cheerful faith in love's power to transform the world.*

—critic Mark Hertsgaard on "All You Need Is Love"

It's like going somewhere without your trousers on.

—John Lennon, describing his life after the death of Brian Epstein

Although they reached a decision shortly after their return, the Beatles did not formally announce the end of their life on the road until November. In the meantime, the band spent several months pursuing separate interests.

Ringo remained content being what he was—a working-class scruff who had the great fortune to become a celebrity. He was happy at home, taking photos and spending time with Maureen and their baby. John went to Spain to film a supporting role in Richard Lester's bitter antiwar comedy, *How I Won the War*. He also began experimenting regularly with LSD and hanging out with London's avant-garde artists.

Paul vacationed in Africa and, back in London, became a regular at gallery openings and concerts. Always the most industrious of the Beatles, McCartney conscientiously began filling in gaps in his knowledge of subjects like music and art, making up for the missing years spent on

Ringo with wife Maureen Cox. Ringo seemed the Beatle least affected by his fame, keeping it in perspective by spending time with his wife and child.

the road. He also wrote the soundtrack for a film, *The Family Way*, and produced records for several acts, including the duo Peter and Gordon. (Peter Asher, Jane's brother, later became a successful producer in his own right.)

George dove deeply into Indian music, specifically north Indian classical music. This interest had been sparked while shooting *Help!*, part of which was set in India. Bored between takes, Harrison had picked up a prop sitar and was instantly attracted to the multistringed instrument's mysterious sound. The more he explored it, the more this music spoke to George—as powerfully as the music of Elvis and Chuck Berry once had. He began studying with a famous sitar player, Ravi Shankar. He also pursued a parallel interest in Indian religion, traveling that fall to India with Pattie to study.

John Lennon in the movie How I Won the War. *Lennon participated in the antiwar comedy in 1966.*

A Troubled Manager

While the Beatles were pursuing individual paths, Brian Epstein was mired in serious problems.

His company was handling several successful Liverpool acts besides the Beatles, including Billy J. Kramer, Cilla Black, and Gerry and the Pacemakers. In time a new associate, Robert Stigwood, added wildly successful acts like the Bee Gees, Cream, and Jimi Hendrix to NEMS's client list. And the Beatles, of course, remained the jewel in Epstein's crown. But as the year drew to a close, he felt the band slipping away from him.

Brian had always felt an almost mystical bond between the band and himself. Managing "the boys" was not a business but almost a holy mission for him. Unfortunately, Epstein was not as brilliant a manager as the Beatles were musicians, and the musicians were painfully aware of it.

Brian was in some ways a very good manager; he had, after all, brought the Beatles to worldwide success. But he lacked the go-for-broke, anything-for-a-buck carnival mentality of someone like Elvis Presley's manager, Colonel Tom Parker. More importantly, he also lacked Parker's ability to create a long-range career plan encompassing all aspects of entertainment.

He was especially poor at tough negotiating. Although the Beatles received the biggest cash advances in history for their

"Music Is Dreams"

Here, George Martin reflects on his creative relationship with the Beatles. The passage is from his book With a Little Help from My Friends.

"My professional life, during the Beatle years, had, of course, one overriding purpose: to make sure the Beatles got what they wanted. I remember a lovely phrase I once heard in a French film, whose title I cannot remember: 'Music is dreams.'

It was their dreams we were realizing: nothing more or less. Music requires mechanics, people banging, or blowing, or scraping, or strumming; but in the end it is intangible, it is dreams. You can't get hold of music, you cannot look at it. You may think you can look at it by picking up a score, but that is just a piece of paper. Music does not exist without a pair of serviceable ears, and time. That is why I think it is the most wonderful art of all—why I get so ecstatic about it. Above all other things, music needs time. . . .

The way we worked, the creative process we always went through, reminds me of a film I once saw of Picasso at work, painting on a ground-glass screen. A camera photographed his brushwork from behind the screen, so that the paint appeared as if by magic. Using time-lapse photography you could see first his original construction, then the complete change as he applied the next layer of paint, then the whole thing revitalized again as he added here, took away there. It reached a point where you thought, 'That's wonderful, for heaven's sake stop!' But he didn't, he went on, and on. Eventually he laid down his brush, satisfied. Or was he? I wonder how many of his paintings he would have wanted to do again. It was a fascinating film of a great artist, of a brilliant creative mind at work. And I have often thought how similar his method of painting was to our way of recording. We, too, would add and subtract, overlaying and underscoring within the limitations of our primitive four-track tape."

1964 American tour, the revenue had barely covered costs. There was also the disastrous affair with Seltaeb ("Beatles" spelled backward). This was a company formed by a friend of Epstein's, Nicky Drake, to market Beatles merchandise.

Seltaeb produced hundreds of thousands of dolls, guitars, wigs, and other gear, each with an "official" Beatles stamp. Unfortunately, before the band became really huge Epstein had signed a contract for a ridiculously low percentage of its profits. His associate at NEMS, Peter Brown, once estimated that Epstein and the band lost about $100 million through this mistake.

All of the Beatles, especially Paul McCartney, were becoming disenchanted with Epstein. They saw their friends, in particular the Rolling Stones, receiving better management and record deals. The Beatles were wealthy enough, but considering the band's vast popularity, there should have been more money pouring in. Epstein knew the band was dissatisfied with his work and could sense them pulling away.

His memoirs are full of sunny lines like, "It's a great privilege being the weatherman, keeping the Beatles and Billy J. and Cilla dry and comfortable."[52] The reality was quite different. On the surface he maintained a sophisticated front, with his handmade suits, immaculate London apartment, and plush suburban home. But he was increasingly moody and withdrawn. He neglected his business to dabble in other enterprises, including a car dealership and a theater, and left much of the day-to-day work to his associates. He rarely came into the office. More and more he indulged in his love of gambling and partying.

On top of it all was Brian's need to maintain secrecy about his sex life. Virtually everyone close to him, including the Beatles, knew that he was gay; it never mattered much to the Beatles, although John's teasing could be cruel. Lennon once suggested that Brian call his memoirs *Queer Jew*—and after the book was published John referred to it mockingly as *A Cellarful of Boys*. Epstein insisted on maintaining an illusion of secrecy. He had good reason; even in the Swinging London of the late 1960s, homosexuality was illegal. Worse, he was lonely; Epstein never found anyone with whom he could have a long-term relationship.

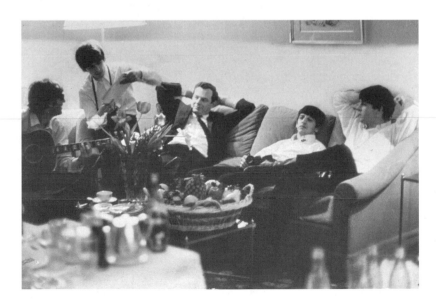

The Beatles and Brian Epstein. The Beatles grew increasingly disenchanted with Epstein's management. Epstein, sensing their disapproval, and with increasing personal problems, grew depressed and suicidal.

Epstein became severely depressed and an insomniac, conditions he fought with a mixture of prescription drugs and drink. Late in 1966 and again in early 1967 he tried to commit suicide by overdosing. In each case, household staff or business associates got him to a hospital in time. After each attempt, Epstein consulted psychiatrists and tried to dry out at private clinics, but his problems only increased.

Leading Up to *Sgt. Pepper*

The Beatles were spending increasingly long periods now to produce songs and increasingly long periods of time on outside interests. As a result, Christmas 1966 was the first Yuletide holiday in years that did not feature a new Beatles album in record stores. In fact, the band's absence from the scene sparked recurrent rumors that they were breaking up.

When the Beatles finally released a new single early in 1967, it was double-sided; that is, Parlophone's marketing department thought both sides were equally strong potential hits. Both focus on memories of Liverpool childhoods, but beyond that the tunes are very different. "Strawberry Fields Forever" is mostly John's—a dreamy, slow song with strange, poetic imagery—while "Penny Lane" is a crisp, lilting song mainly written by Paul.

The songs rank among the Beatles' best, so it was especially disappointing that the record sold poorly. It was the first Beatles single since "Please Please Me" that did not reach number one. The band's unparalleled run of consecutive number-one hits beginning in 1963 ("Please Please Me," "From Me to You," "She Loves You,"

"I Want to Hold Your Hand," "Can't Buy Me Love," "A Hard Day's Night," "I Feel Fine," "Ticket to Ride," "Help!," "Day Tripper," "Paperback Writer," and "Yellow Submarine") was finally broken.

Not only that; the band was beaten out for the number-one slot by Engelbert Humperdinck's ultralight "Release Me." In George Martin's opinion, the fault lay in the marketing. If each song had been released as a single by itself, he wrote, each would have been a smash hit, but by being lumped together the combined sales figures were lower. "It was," Martin noted, "the biggest mistake of my professional life."[53]

Disappointment with the sales record of the single vanished, however, in the wake of that summer's release of the album the Beatles had been working on for so long. Many fans and critics call it the best Beatles record ever. *Sgt. Pepper's Lonely Hearts Club Band* was a triumph in every way—artistic, political, and financial. From the moment of its release in June 1967 it was hailed as the first really important work to come out of pop music, the first creation to successfully merge the energy of rock with the depth of art. It was revolutionary, and it hit the world like a thunderbolt.

Sgt. Pepper

Sgt. Pepper was conceived as a visit to the band's Liverpool childhoods, the idea that had produced the "Strawberry Fields"/"Penny Lane" single. (The single was not included on an album, in keeping with the band's longstanding practice of not making fans pay twice—first for a single and then for an LP—to hear the same song. All the loose Beatles singles have been collected in CD form on the *Past Masters* releases.)

As the new record slowly took shape, the concept changed. The album required seven hundred studio hours over a period of eight months to produce, and it cost

Embracing Psychedelia

Writer Patrick Snyder, in an article reprinted in The Beatles Reader, *comments on the Beatles' embracing of psychedelia and on the power of* Sgt. Pepper.

"Appropriately, their last appearance was in San Francisco . . . the city that had become the focal point of a furious new bubbling in the underground. . . . San Francisco had donned a day-glo striped and strobe-studded cloak and the Beatles followed suit as they prepared to move from the smokey seductiveness of *Revolver* to the piebald pirouetting wonder of *Sgt. Pepper.* . . .

After more months of quiet, at the beginning of the Summer *Newsweek* called Love, it came and everyone followed. With eight Beatles on the cover, *Sgt. Pepper* swept into our lives like a cyclone. The album compelled you to listen in a whole new way because it was a coherent cycle of songs that illuminated a series of interrelated but individually stunning vignettes. It took all of the impulses and emotions that had been stirring in the garrets of New York and the parks of San Francisco and pumped them out into the world. . . .

Without doubt, *Sgt. Pepper* was the most influential record album ever released. In three months, it sold two and a half million copies, permanently changing rock's emphasis from the single to the album, as it cracked open the doors of perception for all those who sat blissfully enthralled in its intricate tapestry of images and sounds. In December of 1967, 60% of American college students identified this album and/or John Lennon as the single most important influence of their lives. From a pop podium of unequaled prominence, the Beatles promulgated [issued] a subversive vision to a ready-made audience of millions of fertile young minds. The result was . . . the same sort of frenzied devotion that had occurred in '64, on a much more sophisticated level."

twenty-five thousand pounds—a huge sum for a pop album at the time and roughly twenty times the cost of the first Beatles album. Eventually it became a mock concert by the fictional Sgt. Pepper.

The songs reflected both the current interests of the Beatles and the prevailing mood in America and England. It was a time of strong passions, and the Beatles responded with strongly passionate music. Protests against the Vietnam War were in full swing. The San Francisco hippie scene had produced the outrageous new style of music called psychedelia. Eastern music and religion were all the rage, and experimentation with mind-expanding drugs was on the rise.

The technical studio achievements of Martin and engineer Geoff Emerick astonished the world, and they are still astonishing—doubly so when we realize that *Sgt. Pepper* was created with monaural four-track tape recorders. Cheerful brass bands, raucous guitars, tapes of antique calliope organ music cut up and randomly spliced together, animal noises, Indian instruments, and string ensembles—all of them blend together brilliantly.

The album has many startling moments. For the climax, "A Day in the Life,"

"This Big White Room"

Quoted in George Martin's book With a Little Help from My Friends, *George Harrison talks about Abbey Road's Studio Two, the unlikely birthplace of the intensely creative* Sgt. Pepper *album.*

"It was all done very clinically, that's the joke. We were in this big white room that was very dirty and hadn't been painted for years, and it had all these old sound baffles hanging down that were all dirty and broken. There was this huge big hanging light, there was no window, no daylight. It was a very clinical, not very nice atmosphere. . . .

In there, we had to make the atmosphere. After a number of years we asked them could we have some coloured lights or a dimmer or something like that; after asking them for about three years, they finally brought in this big steel stand with a couple of red and blue neon lamps on it. That was the magic lighting they gave us. The refrigerator had a padlock on it, so if we wanted a cup of tea we'd have to break open the padlock on the fridge to get the milk out. We had to do that every night for five years. It wasn't like they realized, Oh well, they drink tea after six o'clock, so we'll leave the fridge open, oh no, they padlocked it, all the time. It was weird."

The cover of the Beatles' Sgt. Pepper *album. John Lennon called the album "a peak" in the Beatles' career.*

Lennon told Martin he wanted "a sound building up from nothing to the end of the world."[54] The producer assembled an orchestra, assigned each a low note and a high note, and instructed them to play from one to the other on their own. Another example is the burst of high-pitched sound, too high for the human ear, near the end of the record. George Martin has noted that this was in honor of Paul's dog Martha, and because of its inclusion "more dogs have listened to *Sgt. Pepper* than to any other album in the history of pop music."[55]

As usual, George and Ringo played secondary roles in the album's creation. Harrison wrote only one song, the Indian-influenced "Within You Without You," and Starr spent most of his time waiting to be called into action. As he recalled later, "The biggest memory I have of *Sgt. Pepper* is that I learned to play chess."[56] The drummer had only one vocal, but it

was a prime one: "With a Little Help from My Friends."

By now all four Beatles were experimenting with LSD in addition to their regular marijuana use. Drugs may have affected their business affairs and personal lives, and *Sgt. Pepper* is full of drug references: "I'd love to turn you on," "I get high with a little help from my friends," the teasing title of "Lucy in the Sky with Diamonds." But the band never played stoned. As Ringo recalled years later, "We found out very early on that if you played . . . stoned or derelict in any way it was really shitty music, so we would have the experiences and then bring that into the music later."[57]

The cover of *Sgt. Pepper* was as original as its music. The Beatles and their art director created the cover photo by combining a current craze for military antiques and Victorian relics with images of pop-culture icons: Marilyn Monroe, Marlon

Brando, boxer Sonny Liston, Shirley Temple, and many more. The brilliantly colored jacket was one of the first to use a fold-out, or gatefold, design. Another innovative aspect was the fact that the song lyrics were fully reprinted; today this is common, but *Sgt. Pepper* was the first album to do this.

"All You Need Is Love"

Public reaction to the album was sharply divided. Hippies the world over regarded it as Holy Scripture, full of cosmic messages and prophecies. More conservative Beatle fans bought it in droves, even if they were baffled by the album's psychedelic overtones. It was certified gold—that is, it sold a million copies in America alone—within two weeks of its release.

On the other hand, the BBC banned "A Day in the Life" because of its alleged drug references, and conservative groups on both sides of the Atlantic declared the Beatles to be communists out to brainwash youth. Critics generally loved it: The *London Times* called it "a barometer of our times" and the *New York Times* hailed it as "a new and golden Renaissance of Song." Timothy Leary went even further when he announced, "I declare that the Beatles are mutants. Prototypes of evolutionary agents sent by God with a mysterious power to create a new species."[58]

Throughout the summer the Beatles, resplendent in mustaches and fanciful clothes, threw themselves wholeheartedly into the new culture of peace and love. In June they performed before two hundred million people on one of the world's first large-scale satellite broadcasts, "Our World," to promote international peace. Their song "All You Need Is Love" was written (mainly by John) especially for the show. Its simple, idealistic words perfectly summed up the times, the so-called Summer of Love when young people assured the world that its problems could be solved through peace and love.

The Beatles also publicly announced that all four were involved in Indian religion—specifically, in a system called Transcendental Meditation led by a smiling holy man, Maharishi Mahesh Yogi. Pattie Harrison had been the first in the Beatles circle to be attracted to TM. By August all of the Beatles, plus wives and girlfriends, were attending the Maharishi's lectures in London. At the end of the London session the guru invited his famous guests to a ten-day seminar in Bangor, Wales. The Beatles accepted and asked Brian Epstein to join them. He declined—and so the band took off for Bangor by train, the first big journey the Beatles had made together in years without Brian or a road manager in tow.

The Death of Brian Epstein

That summer the crises in Brian Epstein's life came to a head. His father had recently died. He had sold a majority interest in NEMS, a loss of control Epstein regretted. His attempts to get off pills and drink were failures. He was being blackmailed by an ex-lover. Worst of all, his beloved Beatles were leaving. In October, the five-year contract they had signed in the fall of 1962 would end, and he was certain it would not be renewed. To Epstein, losing the Beatles was as crushing as losing children.

The Beatles sit in the presence of Maharishi Mahesh Yogi, a master of Transcendental Meditation.

While the Beatles were with the Maharishi in Wales at the end of August, Brian Epstein died in his London apartment. Although there was speculation by friends and observers that Epstein may have committed suicide, the official coroner's verdict stated that it was an accidental overdose of sleeping medication.

The Beatles immediately returned to London in a state of shock, confusion, and disbelief. They took the blow extremely hard, despite their new guru's ad-

vice that life was merely an illusion. The musicians were too upset to attend Epstein's funeral, though they sent flowers and attended a memorial service a few weeks later.

The band never fully recovered from Epstein's death. Afterward, they began drifting apart and grew increasingly hostile toward one another. As John Lennon put it years later, "After Brian died we collapsed. . . . We broke up then. That was the disintegration."[59]

9 Drifting Apart

John's in love with Yoko, and he's no longer in love with the three of us.

—Paul McCartney

Immediately following Epstein's death, his brother Clive took over NEMS. Their associate Peter Brown continued to handle the day-to-day affairs. The question of long-term management was unsettled.

Meanwhile, the Beatles agreed to continue work. For some time, Paul had been working on an idea for a film called *Magical Mystery Tour.* Mystery tours are a popular British working-class pastime, in which a group travels by bus to a secret destination. McCartney wrote a minimal screenplay, and in September the band agreed to shoot it, thinking the experience would be fun and therapeutic. And so forty-three people—including actors, journalists, and the Beatles—left London on a hired coach, cameras in hand.

The production was chaotic from beginning to end. No one, least of all the Beatles, had a clear idea of what should happen. The plan was to wander from town to town, filming as events happened. But once the group was out in the countryside, away from familiar London, they realized what a protective shield Brian Epstein had provided for them.

Everywhere they were plagued by journalists, sightseers, and fans. Traffic jams formed as word got out of their movements, and policemen were less than friendly as the bus moved from town to town. They discovered that it was virtually impossible to register a large group at hotels without reservations or even to get proper meals.

The film was as muddled and confused as the production. There was no script, and all the dialogue had been improvised around McCartney's minimal direction. The raw footage was brought back to London and edited by each Beatle separately. Often one would undo what another had done the day before.

The completed hour-long film, which aired just after Christmas on British TV, was the first serious misstep in the Beatles' careers since the disastrous Parisian concerts. Press and public alike hated *Magical Mystery Tour;* typical were the opinions of the London *Daily Express* ("blatant rubbish") and the *Los Angeles Times* (BEATLES BOMB WITH YULE FILM).[60] However, the filmmaking experience did make one thing clear: The strong role Paul McCartney took in masterminding *Magical Mystery Tour* made it clear that he wanted to be the leader of the band.

Apple and India

Rather than look for a strong hand experienced in making and investing money, the Beatles decided over the winter of 1967–68 to do it themselves. Unfortunately, the band's brilliance in the recording studio did not translate to business. Their attempts to manage without outside help were disastrous.

Their first venture was Apple Boutique, an upscale clothing shop in London's Baker Street. Key to this operation was a Dutch collective of psychedelic artists, the Fool. The Fool had already created stage costumes for the Beatles and painted John's Rolls-Royce and George's

"Daddy Has Gone Away Now"

In this transcription of a studio conversation caught on tape and reprinted in Geoffrey Stokes's book The Beatles, *Paul McCartney tries to muster some enthusiasm in his dispirited band.*

"I mean we've been very negative since Mr. Epstein passed away. . . . That's why all of us in turn have been sick of the group, you know. It is a bit of a drag. It's like when you're growing up—your daddy goes away at a certain point in your life and then you stand on your own feet. Daddy has gone away now, you know. I think we either go home, or we do it.

It's discipline we need. Mr. Epstein, he said, 'Get suits on' and we did. And so we were always fighting that discipline a bit. But now it's silly to fight that discipline if it's our own. It's self-imposed these days, so we do as little as possible. But I think we need a bit more if we are going to get on with it."

(Clockwise) Ringo, George, Paul, John, George Martin, and Brian Epstein celebrate in Paris in 1963.

Apple Madness

This selection from Peter Brown's The Love You Make *recalls the crazy ideas and characters that flooded Apple during its heyday.*

"The list of people with schemes and plots and plans is as long as it is sometimes astonishing. There was an American man who wanted the Beatles to purchase anonymously six square miles of Arizona land to hold a three-week rock and roll orgy attended by three million people to climax in a live performance by the Beatles. There was a man with a formula for a pill that could make you into whomever you wanted to be. There were several messiahs and one or two prophets of doom. There was a plan to save whales and a plan to build a commune in India. There was a woman who made tactile art from patent leather covered in oil. There were people who had seen flying saucers and God and needed money to go up, or down, or around in circles. Often they were stopped at Heathrow airport for having no money or passports, and they simply gave John Lennon's or Paul McCartney's name as their sponsor. A family of psychedelized California hippies virtually moved into the Apple building, en route, they said, to the Fiji Islands, and they needed John's aid in setting up a commune. The mother, a fortyish woman named Emily, would blithely breast feed her youngest in the reception room, while a half dozen other totally naked children ran from office to office. The proposals and schemes sent to the office could fill a volume in themselves. They were piled into stacks in a storage closet nicknamed the Black Room, where they threatened to bury anyone who got near them."

fireplace. Now the Beatles gave them a hundred thousand pounds to decorate the boutique and stock it with clothes of the Fool's own design.

John's childhood friend Pete Shotton came from Liverpool, where he had been running a supermarket, to manage the new venture. Another character in the Apple orbit was Magic Alex, a Greek friend of John's who called himself an electronics inventor. Alex was hired to design the boutique's lighting, but soon he was asking for money to finance schemes like a self-dialing phone and a protective force field around the Beatles' houses.

The operations expanded to include Apple Films and Apple Music. These organizations were part of the business empire the Beatles wanted—the first large corporation, the band liked to say, run by young people instead of old men in suits. In interviews, Paul and John referred to this complex scheme as "controlled weirdness" or "a Western Communism" where the band would be free to create within a business environment.

Enormous sums of money began to pour through Apple in pursuit of grandiose plans: a film version of Tolkien's *Lord of the Rings*, a seventy-two-track recording studio designed by Magic Alex, recording contracts for new acts, even no-strings-attached grants to deserving artists. Artists on the new Apple label included singer Mary Hopkin, Badfinger, singer-songwriter James Taylor, and a distinguished jazz group, the Modern Jazz Quartet.

The Beatles continued their involvement with the Maharishi, and in February 1968 a large group—John and Cynthia Lennon, George and Pattie Harrison, Paul McCartney and Jane Asher, Ringo and Maureen Starr, plus Magic Alex and Pattie's sister—made a pilgrimage to India to study with the guru. Other celebrities at the Maharishi's ashram (compound) in Rishekesh included Mike Love of the Beach Boys, British folk rocker Donovan, and actress Mia Farrow.

The Maharishi's lavish compound was not the simple communal life the band had envisioned. Each couple, for instance, had its own luxury cabin. Ringo said it was like Butlin's Holiday Camps, the working-class vacation camps where he had toured with Rory Storm and the Hurricanes. The

drummer, always the least pretentious Beatle, brought along a suitcase of baked beans because Indian food didn't agree with him—and he couldn't wait to get home. After only ten days, Ringo and Maureen returned to London and their children.

The other band members also began to lose their illusions about the Maharishi, especially after they proposed that he star in a film. The supposed holy man, whom they had thought was uninterested in material things, proved to be very tough when the talk turned to royalties. The final straw came when the guru made sexual advances toward Mia Farrow. According to

The Beatles gradually grew disenchanted with the Maharishi, especially when it became clear that his interests were more material than spiritual.

John, the group converged on the Maharishi's "very rich-looking bungalow in the mountains" to announce their departure. When the guru asked why, Lennon replied, "Well, if you're so cosmic, you'll know why." John recalled that "he gave me a look like 'I'll kill you, you bastard' and . . . I knew then . . . I had called his bluff."[61] Back in England, Paul told reporters, "We made a mistake. We thought there was more to him than there was."[62]

Enter Yoko and Linda

Throughout these exciting but confusing times, two women were becoming important figures in the Beatles' universe. Yoko Ono and Linda Eastman have both been accused of breaking up "the world's most exclusive boy's club," of destroying a legendary friendship and a unique partnership. Although Ono and Eastman did play roles in alienating the Beatles from each other, many other factors also contributed to the group's dissolution.

One way John coped with his chronic restlessness and his stagnant marriage was by indulging his interest in avant-garde art, and he frequently attended chic gallery openings. At London's tiny Indica Gallery, he observed a show called "Unfinished Paintings and Objects." The artist was Yoko Ono.

Ono, the daughter of a well-to-do Japanese family, was an American citizen who had been living in London since 1966 with her husband and daughter. She already had a strong reputation as an avant-garde artist in both England and America. At her first meeting with Lennon in the Indica Gallery in 1966, Ono walked over to the famous guest and handed him a card on which was printed the single word "Breathe." He responded by panting like a dog.

Yoko, John, and son Julian. The entrance of Yoko into John's life would affect all of the Beatles.

Photographer Linda Eastman would become Paul's wife. She and Yoko Ono were both accused of "breaking up" the Beatles.

It was the beginning of a love affair that would continue until Lennon's death, although at first the connection was purely intellectual. John was fascinated with Yoko's unconventional ideas about art and by her intense personality. He also liked the fact that she knew nothing about rock and so was unimpressed with his fame. Their relationship quickly intensified, though it would not become physical for several years.

Meanwhile, a new woman was entering Paul McCartney's life. His longtime girlfriend, Jane Asher, was a successful actress; in fact, she was the only Beatle wife or sweetheart who was in the spotlight on her own. Cynthia Lennon, Maureen Starr, and Pattie Harrison had all been content to stay in the shadows of their famous spouses. As Pattie once told reporters, "A Beatle wife is just baggage. There's no pretending any different."[63]

As time went on, McCartney and Asher began having difficulty maintaining a relationship in light of their dual careers; neither was willing to compromise. Paul began dating other women, relishing his role as the only bachelor Beatle. No one became important to him, however, until he met Linda Eastman during the *Sgt. Pepper* sessions. The daughter of a prominent New York lawyer who specialized in music copyrights, Linda was a photographer and a regular companion of an international set of rock stars. They began seeing each other regularly, and by the time Paul returned from India she was a major part of his life.

The next Beatles single, "Hey Jude," echoed the romantic problems of Paul and his friend John. Paul had begun the ballad as "Hey Julian," a song meant to comfort John's son while the young boy coped with his parents' problematic marriage. McCartney realized later that its lyrics also reflected his own uncertain love life. John Lennon, meanwhile, interpreted the song as encouragement for himself and Yoko. After its release in August 1968, "Hey Jude" became the band's most successful single, selling over 3 million copies, as well as the longest single ever released; at over seven minutes in length, it was radically longer than any other pop single to date.

The *White Album*

In May 1968 the Beatles started work on their first album for Apple. The band had a lot of material written during their stay in India—enough to make a double LP, an unusual concept at the time. This record is generally called the *White Album*, in honor of its stark cover, though its official title is *The Beatles*. The simple title was meant to indicate unity, but the album revealed the band's tensions and problems. *The Beatles* is a collection of songs by individual singers with backing.

One major problem during the sessions at Abbey Road was the constant presence of Yoko Ono, who was now John's full-time companion. Lennon insisted that she be at his side. It was the first time anyone had been allowed into the recording circle besides George Martin, the engineers, Neil Aspinall and Mal Evans, and the Beatles themselves. At first the others were not upset, figuring that Ono was simply the latest of John's enthusiasms; one reason the Beatles had been able to stay friends for so long, after all, was their tolerance of one another's quirks. But as time went on and the tiny, black-clad Yoko clung on—she never left John's side, even when he went to the bathroom—the tension mounted.

This tension can be heard in the album's disjointed songs. By now, John and Paul were rarely working together, and the differences between their styles is obvious. Lennon's contributions, including "Revolution," "Happiness Is a Warm Gun," and "Sexy Sadie" (a song about the Maharishi), are edgy and provocative, showing the influence of Yoko Ono but lacking McCartney's charm. Paul's songs, including "Martha My Dear," "Rocky Raccoon," and "Blackbird," are even sweeter than usual, without Lennon's balancing cynicism.

Occasionally, McCartney and Lennon stepped outside these roles; Paul's "Helter Skelter" is close to heavy metal, while songs like "Julia" showed that John could be tenderly melodic. Meanwhile, George Harrison contributed several songs, the best being "While My Guitar Gently Weeps" with his friend Eric Clapton soloing—virtually the first solo on a Beatle record by anyone other than the Beatles or George Martin.

Ringo was sidelined even more than usual. At one point he became so dispirited that he quit the band; Paul had to play drums on "Back in the U.S.S.R." in his absence. The others were able to coax Ringo back after a week. When he returned to Abbey Road, his drum kit had been covered with flowers by the others.

Two Virgins

Also in 1968 the Beatles recorded songs for an animated feature, *Yellow Submarine*. This is a charming pop-art full-length cartoon that features caricatures of the Beatles and frequent references to their songs. The only direct connection the Beatles had to *Yellow Submarine* besides the new songs was a brief live appearance at the end. The movie was useful to them, however, because it fulfilled the three-movie contract they had with their film studio.

Personal problems were taking up most of the band's time—especially John Lennon's. In October, Cynthia filed for divorce and John and Yoko were arrested for marijuana possession. The Beatles had publicly announced they were giving up drugs, though George was the only one who had completely renounced all drugs and alcohol in keeping with his Indian religious practices. In fact, John and Yoko (who was pregnant) had begun experimenting with heroin, although none was found when they were arrested. They eventually pleaded guilty and paid a small fine.

The following month, on the day the *White Album* was released, Ono and Lennon released a collaborative record, *Unfinished Music No. 1: Two Virgins.* The cover showed the couple facing the camera, arms around each other and completely nude. The head of EMI Records, Sir Joseph Lockwood, refused to release it. When Yoko replied that it was art, Sir Joseph shot back, "In that case, why not show Paul in the nude? He's so much better looking."[64] A compromise was eventually reached and the records were wrapped in brown paper.

On the day of the album's release, Yoko suffered a miscarriage. The couple turned even this personal tragedy into art; the dying baby's heartbeat was recorded for their next record, *Unfinished Music No. 2: Life with the Lions.* Lennon and Ono saw these albums as a diary. John told reporters he hoped they would form a series "that will go on for the rest of our lives.

We'd like to be able to produce them as fast as newspapers and television can. It will be a constant autobiography of our life together."[65]

Apple Dissolves

Through the summer and fall the other Beatles were having problems as well—especially with Apple Corps, as the group's business entity was now known. Things were completely out of control. Shoplifting from the boutique had long been rampant. When even the clerks began stealing, the Beatles decided to close the boutique in a typically flamboyant way, by giving everything away. They opened the doors to the public and announced that everything was free. Within a few hours the clothes, the fixtures, and even parts of the walls had disappeared.

Apple Corps's new offices in Savile Row, meanwhile, were just as chaotic. TV

Customers crowd the closing of the Apple boutique in order to take advantage of the free merchandise.

sets, stereos, and other equipment were disappearing at a rapid rate. Dozens of staffers were drawing huge salaries and producing nothing. One office was occupied by an astrologer who prepared daily horoscopes for everyone and guided business policy by referring to such mystical sources as the *I Ching*. Magic Alex's state-of-the-art studio in the basement was an especially bad disaster: It had store-bought tape machines, not the seventy-two-track wizardry he had promised, allowed the noise of the building's furnace to seep through, and was so poorly designed that there was not even an intercom between the control booth and the studio.

Everyone at Apple was wandering around in a daze, unwilling to take responsibility for anything. The reception room was filled with people hoping to get a piece of the action. Among them were American Hell's Angels gang members invited by George. After bringing themselves, their women, and their motorcycles to London at Apple's expense, the Angels terrorized everyone before announcing that they were on their way to Czechoslovakia "to straighten out the political situation there." Another hanger-on was a man who wanted fifty thousand pounds because, as Apple press agent Derek Taylor put it,

> he now was all of the people mentioned in both *Sgt. Pepper's Lonely Hearts Club Band* and in [Bob Dylan's album] *John Wesley Harding* and in addition he is Popeye the Sailor Man and he needs every penny he can get to act out this amalgam in a movie.[66]

Clearly, help was needed. The head of one of England's largest merchant banks offered to salvage the company at no fee, but the Beatles didn't respond. Instead, they turned to two others, Allen Klein and Lee Eastman. The rivalry between these men to become the manager of the world's biggest rock band would soon play a major part in that band's breakup.

Chapter

10 The Breakup

People keep talking about it as if it's the end of the world. It's only a rock band. You have all the old records if you want to reminisce.

—John Lennon

Nah. But if we did, we wouldn't be so bitchy about it.

—Mick Jagger, when asked if the Rolling Stones would ever break up

On top of the Beatles' other problems was a lack of musical direction. Paul was urging a return to their first love, live performance. The others were not enthusiastic, however; they wanted no part of anything like Beatlemania.

They eventually reached a compromise: an album that resembled a live show in simplicity and directness. They saw it as a return to the basics of performance, without fancy effects.

The working title was *Get Back*—a reference both to a song of Paul's and to a return to basics. All the rehearsals and recording sessions would be filmed to create a feature-length documentary.

The work began early in 1969, not in the familiar atmosphere of Abbey Road or in Magic Alex's still-unfinished studio but in a huge, drafty movie soundstage outside London. This was so that the film's director, Michael Lindsay-Hogg, could move his crew around more easily. Paul was like a

cheerleader in his efforts to get the others motivated, but the sessions did not go smoothly. No one liked playing in the freezing studios. None of the songwriters had strong material. Instead they played a lot of old songs from their Hamburg days, along with early Lennon-McCartney tunes like "The One After 909." And tension between the band members quickly reappeared.

The group in the early days. As the Beatles tried to work together on a live album in 1969, their differences and animosities became more pronounced.

Things were especially strained between George and Paul. Harrison was bitter about what he saw as poor treatment. "I'll play whatever you want me to play," George sarcastically told Paul at one point. "Or I won't play at all. Whatever it is that'll please you, I'll do it."[67] A few days into the sessions, George left in disgust. The others coaxed him back, as they had Ringo, but the tensions were unresolved.

The film studios were a failure, but by that time Abbey Road had already been

---

Killing the King

In an interview published in Newsweek *in October 1980, less than two months before his death, John Lennon reflects on how Yoko Ono brought him out of the doldrums he was experiencing as a jaded rock star.*

"I was used to a situation where the newspaper was there for me to read, and after I'd read it, somebody else could have it. . . . I think that's what kills people like Presley and others of that ilk. . . . The king is always killed by his courtiers, not by his enemies. The king is overfed, over-drugged, overindulged, anything to keep the king tied to his throne. Most people in that position never wake up. They either die mentally or physically or both. And what Yoko did for me . . . was to liberate me from that situation. And that's how the Beatles ended. Not because Yoko split the Beatles, but because she showed me what it was to be Elvis Beatle and to be surrounded by syco-phants and slaves who are only interested in keeping the situation as it was. And that's a kind of death."

Yoko fostered John's already growing disillusionment with the Beatles, allowing him to break away and take more interest in his own independent projects.

Paul and Linda are mobbed by well-wishers after their wedding ceremony in 1969.

booked by other artists. The band moved instead into Apple's basement with rented equipment. An American keyboardist, Billy Preston, was also brought in. Preston, an excellent musician and a cheerful person, helped put the others on their best behavior. The band forged ahead and recorded over a hundred songs, originals and covers, and the film crew recorded about thirty hours of footage. But no one felt that the music was good enough to be released.

In the meantime, they had been unable to agree on a location for the concert that would be the film's climax. Various locations were proposed, including an amphitheater in Tunisia and a giant ship at sea. John suggested an insane asylum, which he thought expressed the madness of the undertaking. In the end, for lack of anything better, the Beatles simply hauled equipment to the top of Apple's building in Savile Row. This spontaneous rooftop show lasted until policemen, responding to complaints, shut it down.

That spring, while going back and forth about what to do with the raw *Get Back* tapes, the top Beatles reached decisions about their personal lives. On March 12, Paul McCartney married Linda Eastman at a London registry. Linda's daughter by a previous marriage was the flower girl and a handful of friends and family members attended. No other Beatles were present. The loss of the only bachelor Beatle devastated females around the world; dozens camped out on McCartney's doorstep as the McCartneys retreated to the remote farm in Scotland Paul owned.

Eight days later, John Lennon married Yoko Ono at the British embassy on the island of Gibraltar. Some see this as another aspect of the intense rivalry between John and Paul; John seemed incapable of letting Paul take the spotlight without doing something attention-getting himself. Unlike Paul and Linda, John and Yoko had a very public honeymoon. They spent seven days in bed at the Amsterdam Hilton in what they called a bed-in for peace. The

John and Yoko speak from their bed at the Amsterdam Hilton while on their televised honeymoon in 1969.

press mostly scoffed at the gesture, pointing out the irony of campaigning for peace from a bed in a luxury hotel. Typical of the headlines was this mocking one: DAY TWO OF THE LENNON LIE-IN: JOHN AND YOKO ARE FORCED OUT BY MARIA THE MAID.[68]

John and Yoko remained highly visible political activists and artists. After years of hiding his anger at social injustices and his frustration with being a Beatle, Lennon was letting his wild side emerge. Among other things, the couple released hundreds of white "balloons for peace," appeared onstage inside a giant bag, cut off their hair and donated it to the Black Panther Party, and sent acorns to world leaders as a peace gesture. Many fans were dismayed by Lennon's harsh manner; they worried that Ono's influence had sent him over the edge of sanity. The London *Daily Mirror*, echoing this sentiment,

called him "a not inconsiderable talent who seems to have gone completely off his rocker."[69]

Abbey Road

A number of landmark events occurred during the summer of 1969. Neil Armstrong became the first person to walk on the moon. The Woodstock festival gathered half a million people in a messy, anarchic, idealistic event that symbolized the hippie era. A charismatic man named Charles Manson and his followers murdered actress Sharon Tate and several others in a horrifying rampage that Manson said was inspired by two Beatles songs, "Helter Skelter" and "Piggies." But it was also the summer of one last Beatle album.

The music of *Get Back* was on hold while the film was being edited. In the meantime, Paul was eager to make another album, and in July he approached George Martin. Martin was reluctant after the disappointing *Get Back* sessions, but Paul persuaded him to give the band one more try—and somehow convinced the other Beatles as well. The four spent the rest of that summer creating the glorious *Abbey Road*.

Unlike the *White Album* and *Get Back*, *Abbey Road* was a marvel of cooperation and inspiration. The songs perfectly balanced John's bitterness with Paul's sweetness; the production balanced the band's early simplicity with their later sophistication. George Harrison reached a high new level of songwriting, and the sound quality—since *Abbey Road* was the first and only Beatles LP recorded on eight-track machines—was a triumph for George Martin.

There was still tension among the Beatles, but no one would have guessed from listening to *Abbey Road*. Critics and fans responded with equal enthusiasm to the record's fresh sound when it was released in September, and it sold over five million copies within a year. Part of the reason for the album's strong sales was a bizarre rumor that surfaced after its release that Paul was dead. This strange tale began as a joke and escalated into an elaborate hoax; from there it passed into pop-culture legend.

"Paul Is Dead"

The story began with a mock review in a college newspaper in Ann Arbor, Michigan. The piece claimed that evidence of McCartney's demise could be found in clues on the cover of *Abbey Road*. The photo of the musicians walking across the street represented Paul's funeral: John, in a white suit, was the minister; dark-suited Ringo, the undertaker; George, in denims, was the gravedigger. Paul himself was barefoot, out of step with the other three and holding a cigarette in his right hand although he was left-handed. The clincher was a Volkswagen Beetle in the background with the license plate 28 IF— Paul's age *if* he were alive.

Despite the flimsy evidence (Paul was twenty-seven, for one thing; for another, he only played the bass left-handed and old photos often show him holding a cigarette in his right hand), the rumor quickly spread and was soon embellished to ridiculous proportions. Various versions

---

Scaling the Peaks One Last Time

Writer Mark Hertsgaard, in this excerpt from his book A Day in the Life, *remarks on the Beatles' rooftop concert in the film* Let It Be *and the final days of the band.*

"The inside jokes, the wacky wordplay, the gleeful nose-thumbing at authority—it almost seemed as if the intervening years of glory and madness had somehow fallen away and the Beatles were back at the Cavern Club, four young phenoms out to conquer the world and have a rocking good time doing it.

Yet by the time *Let It Be* was actually released, on May 13, 1970, the Beatles had passed irrevocably into history. Those four young phenoms had indeed conquered the world and had lots of fun along the way, but after 'having scaled every known peak of show business, [they] quite deliberately never came home again,' as McCartney phrased it in a mock press release he read during the shooting of the film."

claimed that he was murdered by the CIA, that he had been decapitated in a car accident, that an actor named William Campbell had undergone plastic surgery to become his double.

Dozens of other "clues" were soon discovered in earlier Beatle albums. Scraps of noise, *Sgt. Pepper*'s Billy Shears, and lines from "A Day in the Life" and "I Am the Walrus" all allegedly bolstered the theory by supplying hidden "proof" of McCartney's death. One of the most famous of these bogus clues claimed that John's chant of "number nine" during "Revolution 9" on the *White Album*, played backward, revealed the words, "Turn me on, dead man."

"Paul is dead" magazines and TV documentaries appeared—even morbid records with titles like *Saint Paul, Dear Paul, The Ballad of Paul,* and *Paulbearer.* As the rumors grew in intensity, *Life* magazine reporters tracked McCartney to Scotland, where he had secluded himself after *Abbey Road* wrapped up. McCartney offered them an interview and a chance to photograph the

Misunderstood

In this interview from the 1980s, reprinted in The Lost Beatles Interviews, *Paul McCartney discusses his long feud with John Lennon.*

"Well, like anyone I wouldn't mind being understood rather than misunderstood. It's very tempting when someone like John was slagging me off in the press . . . to answer back, but I'm glad I didn't. I just thought the hell with it, he's going over the top like he does. He was a great fella, but he had that about him. He'd suddenly throw the table over and on to a new thing. And I was the table. But, I mean, a lot of it was talk and I think John loved the group. I think, though, he had to clear the decks for his new life. . . .

But I don't think I was the bad guy or the good guy. I think originally what happened is that I'm from a very close, warm family in Liverpool, and I was very lucky to come from that kind of family. John wasn't. John was an only child. His father left home [when John was] three. His mother was killed when he was sixteen. My mum died when I was fourteen, so we had that in common. But when it came to meet the press and I saw a guy in the outer office shaking, I'd go in and say, 'Want a cup of tea?' because I just didn't like to be around that tension, that nervousness. So it fell to me to go and chat to the guy and put him at ease."

newest McCartney, infant Mary, in an effort to squelch the rumors. Borrowing a line from Mark Twain, Paul breezily told them, "The rumors of my death have been greatly exaggerated. However, if I was dead, I'm sure I'd be the last to know."[70]

A Divorce

In the battle over who would become the manager of the Beatles, on one side was a rumpled-looking New Yorker, Allen Klein. Klein was a former accountant who had made fortunes for performers as diverse as Bobby Darin, Sam Cooke, the Rolling Stones, and Donovan. He had been trying to convince the Beatles since 1966 to let him negotiate them a better record deal. Although the band far outpaced any other in record sales, they made less than they could have because Brian Epstein had never asked for advance money—a guarantee against future record sales—from EMI.

John liked Klein's blunt style, and he had been strongly in favor of hiring him after Epstein's death; George and Ringo were willing to go along. But after Paul became involved with Linda Eastman, he urged the others to choose Linda's father, Lee, the New York lawyer, instead. Eastman's expertise in music copyright law was in his favor, but his personal relationship with Paul was not to the other Beatles' liking. In part, it came down to a war of style: Klein's street-fighting ways versus Eastman's elegant Wall Street manners. It did not help things that the two men could barely stand each other.

The situation became critical while Lennon and McCartney were on their honeymoons. A huge entertainment company, ATV, tried to buy Northern Music, which published the duo's songs, from their longtime publisher, Dick James. The venture was perfectly legal, but John and Paul were furious; to them, selling the rights to their songs was treason. The Beatles hired Klein to help them fight the move and to put Apple's affairs in order. However, McCartney refused to sign a long-term agreement with Klein.

Meanwhile, Lennon was busy waging peace. Just before the release of *Abbey Road*, John and Yoko were invited to attend a benefit concert for peace in Toronto, Canada. It was short notice—the concert was the following day—but John impulsively decided to go if he could perform. Within hours he had pulled together an impromptu band: himself, Yoko, Eric Clapton, bassist Klaus Voorman, and drummer Alan White.

A charter airplane was hurriedly booked and the following day, with minimal rehearsal, the Plastic Ono Band played in Toronto. One of the new songs Lennon performed was "Cold Turkey," which appeared on the album *Live Peace in Toronto* early in 1970. It was the first song John Lennon ever recorded or published without a cocredit to Paul McCartney.

He had written "Cold Turkey" as a song about withdrawing from heroin, a process he had recently undergone. But it can also be heard as a song about the equally addictive state of Beatlehood, for John was increasingly unhappy in that role. He was tired of the bickering and frustrated by artistic differences. For the first time, he was talking about splitting up the band he had started so long ago. En route home from Toronto, John made his decision: He no longer wanted to be a Beatle.

John and Yoko perform with their band, the Plastic Ono Band, in 1969.

At a group meeting soon after, Paul proposed that they tour England and play small clubs unannounced. George and Ringo were willing to give this scheme a try, but John told them they were crazy. He then announced flatly that he wanted "a divorce, like my divorce from Cynthia."[71]

The rest of the band was saddened but not especially surprised at this; for months, John had been pulling away. Still, it was a blow to a group of friends who had once been so close. As Paul later put it, the others felt they could hardly blame John for wanting to move on:

> He wanted to live life, do stuff, and there was no holding back with John. And it was what we all admired him for. So we couldn't really say: "Oh, we don't want you to do that, John. Stay with us." You'd feel so wimpy. It *had* to happen.[72]

Lennon agreed to keep the news of his departure quiet for the time being, to protect a deal that Allen Klein was negotiating for them with Capitol. After John left the meeting, the others agreed that this would probably be just a temporary halt; they knew John and his temper, and they felt sure that he would cool off and change his mind in time.

"I Read the News Today, Oh Boy"

It was not temporary; the Beatles dissolved slowly and painfully over the next several months. The band had always wanted to go out while on top of the heap and, in Paul's words, "leave 'em laughing."[73] When the end finally came, however, they were unprepared. They had

On the Wind-Swept Roof

This excerpt from Chet Flippo's Yesterday *reflects on the Beatles' final rooftop concert and the role each musician seemed to have slipped into by then.*

"The Beatles were dead long before Paul led them—almost, it seemed, against their will—up on to the wind-swept roof of Apple that frigid January 30, 1969. For their final public hurrah, the four Beatles finally resembled the individuals that they were growing into. At their previous Last Concert, the August 29, 1966, farewell in Candlestick Park in San Francisco, they had still been the Fab Four, object of teen dreams on an unprecedented scale, global mass hysteria, and moist underwear. Since then they had undergone LSD, *Sgt. Pepper,* worldwide cult-status, and a startling introduction to the bizarre world of global business and finances attendant to being a Social Phenomenon. . . .

Small wonder that they started to grow protective shells. At the close of 1968, John was twenty-eight years old, Paul was twenty-six, George was twenty-six, and Ringo was twenty-eight. Except for Paul, they had no illusions left for Beatledom. George and Ringo had been treated as second-class session men for so long that they grew to know their place. . . . And John—well, he was John and he would do as he damned well pleased—after checking with Yoko, that is. Yoko, who was new to the Beatle scene, was hovering on the periphery of this action. So was Linda Eastman, for that matter.

But up on the Apple roof, the Beatles were the Beatles for the last time ever in public view. They—ever so briefly—reveled in performing once again. George, with his high-top black Converse sneakers and rakish mustache, evoked the image of his black-leather delinquent adolescence. John, long-haired and dressed all in black, played his hollow-body Gibson with rare abandon. Ringo was—well, he was Ringo, which is all anyone ever asked of him. But Paul was all business. He was full-bearded then and seemed to gain confidence with the long hair and whiskers and somber suit and hiking boots he wore. As Head Beatle, he was completely oblivious to what the others felt, wanted, needed, or even perceived."

no emotional, legal, or financial plans for dissolution—they never thought it could really happen. And so when it came it was a messy, ugly affair, indeed very much like a divorce.

That winter they maintained separate lives. George's appetite for playing live had been whetted by Paul's proposal, and he toured America backing the singers Delaney and Bonnie Bramlett in a band that included Eric Clapton. Ringo maintained his movie career, costarring with Peter Sellers in a black comedy called *The Magic Christian*. The drummer also worked on his first solo album, a collection of old songs called *Sentimental Journey*. Paul began work on a solo album but remained a recluse in Scotland.

Although the Beatles' breakup has been attributed to numerous causes, perhaps the most obvious is that the "boys" simply grew up to be very different men.

John was still the Beatle most in the public eye, including a renunciation of his MBE. Lennon took the medal from its place atop his Aunt Mimi's television set and returned it to Buckingham Palace to protest, he said, atrocities in Vietnam and Biafra and, in a sour joke, also the failure of "Cold Turkey" to remain in the British top twenty.

In the early spring of 1970, Paul returned to London and contacted John after a silence between them of nearly six months. Paul informed his friend that he was releasing his own record and, at the same time, leaving the group. "Good," John coolly replied. "That makes two of us who have accepted it mentally."[74] Paul further said he planned to release *McCartney* in April. The others protested, arguing that it would clash with the release both of Ringo's solo LP and with the long-delayed *Let It Be* album.

They tried to contact Paul, but he was unavailable. Ringo personally went to Paul's London house, but McCartney lost his temper with the drummer. Ringo, genuinely shocked, persuaded the others to let Paul have his way, since it was obviously an emotional issue for him. The release date for Ringo's solo album was brought forward to March, the date for *Let It Be* was pushed back to May, and *McCartney* came out as scheduled on April 17.

With it came the first public acknowledgment that the Beatles were breaking up. Included with *McCartney* was a mock interview Paul wrote himself, in which he stated that the band was splitting up, perhaps temporarily. The self-interview, released a week before the album, was taken by the press as official. John had stuck with his bargain to keep his own departure quiet; now Paul's announcement made it seem as though he had been the first to make the move.

Let It Be

The news stunned people around the world. Reporters everywhere scrambled to sort out conflicting stories and rumors. The Apple press office was officially denying the breakup. George told reporters that it was true but only temporary. John discussed the breakup in *Rolling Stone* magazine as if it were permanent.

As the rumors continued to swirl, the *Let It Be* album was released with advance orders of nearly 4 million in the United States alone. Despite the strong sales, the album was one of the weakest the band ever made—a sad final note for a band that had once set the standard. Not one of the Beatles was satisfied with *Let It Be*.

In large part, this was due to the loss of George Martin's guiding hand. After months of neglect, the *Get Back* tapes had been turned over by Klein to the legendary American producer Phil Spector. In the late 1950s and early 1960s, Spector had created dozens of hits using a lush style called the wall of sound. He had once influenced the Beatles deeply, and in his own way was brilliant—but he was a spectacularly bad choice to produce a simple, no-frills rock album. The end result, with its overdubbed choirs and string sections, was a long way from what the band had initially conceived.

The film version of *Let It Be* was released at the same time. Like the album, it was mostly a mess—a confused documentary about a once-powerful and focused group that had lost its direction

Burning Down the Factory

Writer Mark Hertsgaard, in this passage from A Day in the Life, *reflects on how their audience contributed to the band's breakup.*

"It was not entirely their own fault. The adoring millions also played a part. Like moths to a flame, the Beatles' fans were ineluctably [irresistibly] drawn to the four young men whose music and charisma made everyone feel so happy and alive. By overwhelming their heroes with the intensity and relentlessness of their passion, however, the fans ended up driving the Beatles into seclusion and, ultimately, retirement.

As Harrison later said, in the best single explanation of why the Beatles finally decided to 'burn down the factory' that was their collective identity, 'It's just that it wasn't as much fun for us in the end as it was for all of you.' Denying that Yoko and Linda were responsible for breaking up the Beatles, Ringo commented years later that, 'From 1961, 1962 to around 1969, we [the four Beatles] were just all for each other. But suddenly you're older and you don't want to devote all that time to this one object. . . . We stopped because we'd had enough. We'd gone as far as we could with each other.' George, too, referred to the Beatles experience as 'stifling,' adding that it finally came to resemble a situation where 'you've got ten brothers and sisters and you've grown up and you're all forty years old and you still haven't moved out. . . . We had to try to help break that Beatle madness in order to have space to breathe, to become sort of human.'"

and energy. *Let It Be* was supposed to be a film about the making of an album; instead, it was a portrait of the dissolution of a band, a picture of friendship gone sour. The British newspaper *New Musical Express* called it "a sad and tatty [ragged] end to a musical fusion which wiped clean and drew again the face of pop music."[75]

Still, the record and film have some wonderful moments. One of the best—a moment that evokes all the overflowing wit and energy the band once possessed—comes at the end of their impromptu concert on the Apple roof. After their final number, "Get Back," John Lennon steps to the microphone and dryly announces, "I'd like to say thank you very much on behalf of the group and myself . . . and I hope we passed the audition."[76]

After the Beatles

The Beatles are for the history books, like the year 1492.

—George Harrison

We gave everything for ten years. We gave ourselves. If we played now, anyway, we'd just be four rusty old men.

—John Lennon on reunion offers

Life went on for the Fab Four after the breakup, but it was very different.

Ringo, the low-key, kindly man John Lennon once called "quite simply the heart of the Beatles,"[77] continues to cheerfully enjoy his unexpected fame. He established residency in Monaco for tax purposes and became a regular on the international jet-set circuit, showing up at celebrity functions around the world. He remarried; has made occasional albums and movies (notably the album *Ringo* and the movie *That'll Be the Day*, both released in 1973); and has mounted a few tours with a celebrity-studded group called the All-Starr Band. He even reached a new audience of very young people through his role as Mr. Conductor on the children's public-television show *Shining Time Station*.

George, still bitter toward Lennon and McCartney, celebrated his release from restrictive "junior Beatledom" by recording a fine three-record set, *All Things Must Pass*, although his subsequent records have tended toward dullness. He also organized a massive benefit show and album, *The*

George sings during The Concert for Bangladesh *in 1972.*

Concert for Bangladesh; toured briefly; married a second time; and financed many films, including *The Rutles: All You Need Is Cash,* a brilliant pseudodocumentary parody of Beatlemania. Indian religion remains an important part of his life.

As for the driving forces in the band, Lennon and McCartney's solo music never hit the peaks they had reached as a team. Their records sold well but were generally lacking. McCartney's work was seen as hopelessly trivial; one English newspaper wrote about Paul's second solo LP, *Ram:* "How do you tell an ex-Beatle that he has made a lousy album?" Lennon's music was generally stronger, but his obsessions with psychotherapy and politics made his albums painfully stark. As a *Rolling Stone* critic wrote about Lennon's LP *Imagine,* "I fear that John sees himself in the role of the truth-teller, and as such can justify any kind of self-indulgent brutality in the name of truth."[78]

Paul McCartney's solo releases, both with Wings (the band he formed after the Beatles' breakup) and under his own name, have rarely been as strong as his prime Beatle work. (One exception is the fine *Tug of War,* produced by his old chum George Martin.) But Paul has in many ways proved to be the sturdiest and most reliable of all the ex-Beatles. Even his weakest records sell phenomenally well, and he has fruitfully collaborated with such gifted artists as Michael Jackson, Stevie Wonder, and Elvis Costello. All along, he has stubbornly continued to write (and believe in) songs that reflect his sunny, optimistic outlook.

In addition to McCartney's recordings, he has been massively successful in other ways. His regular world tours have made him the most visible ex-Beatle. He has

Paul remains the most musically prolific and financially successful Beatle. While many believe Paul's music to be silly and light, others continue to appreciate his sunny view.

invested his money wisely and is one of the wealthiest musicians in the world. His marriage appears to be happy, the McCartney family has expanded to include four children, and he and Linda have become outspoken advocates of vegetarianism and animal rights. There have been a few bumps in the road, notably marijuana busts in America and Japan and criticism of his decision to include Linda (a modest singer and musician) in his bands; generally, however, McCartney's path has been as smoothly cheerful as his boyish public persona.

John Lennon's road was rockier. He and Yoko moved to New York City in 1971, primarily to pursue custody of Kyoko, Yoko's daughter. At first denied entry to the United States because of his drug conviction, Lennon found he could enter the country for specialized medical treatment. He and Yoko began a radical form of therapy called primal screaming. Through it, Lennon could both explore the tangled psychology of his childhood and live in the States legally.

The Lennons settled into Manhattan's ornate Dakota Apartments. They unsuc-cessfully pursued their custody case but successfully fought an effort by President Nixon's administration to deport the musician. After their son, Sean, was born, John retired and spent his time caring for the baby. In the midseventies the couple separated and John spent a year in Los Angeles on an extended binge. He then declared that "the separation didn't take," moved back to the Dakota, began a strict macrobiotic diet, and gave up drugs and alcohol. In the late 1970s he entered a new phase of creativity, released an excellent record with Yoko, *Double Fantasy*, and tentatively renewed his long-soured friendships with the other Beatles. Then, on

---

The Beatles and Mozart

In a 1992 interview, Paul McCartney remarked, "A hundred years from now, people will listen to the music of the Beatles the same way we listen to Mozart." Writer Mark Hertsgaard, in his critical study A Day in the Life, *adds this comment:*

"When Paul McCartney says that . . . he isn't—or shouldn't be—claiming that the Beatles are Mozart's musical equals. Comparing Mozart and the Beatles is, in that sense, like comparing apples and oranges. But the Beatles may well be regarded as the twentieth-century counterpart of Mozart. Like him, they created music that was not only the most popular of its time but also of the very highest quality artistically."

Paul McCartney

December 8, 1980, Lennon was shot to death outside his building by a psychotic fan, Mark David Chapman.

The tragedy, of course, devastated the surviving Beatles. It also cut short any possibility of a reunion, a hope voiced regularly by fans, promoters, and even the secretary-general of the United Nations, who had once asked them to unite for a benefit concert. Shaken but undeterred, Beatles fans and entrepreneurs maintained the countless conventions, fan magazines, tribute shows, and other activities that keep the group's name alive. Their record company, meanwhile, continues to produce remastered CD reissues and compilations of their always popular work.

The Beatles never faded from the public eye, although since their breakup they have had two especially prominent periods: one in the wake of their 1988 induction into the Rock and Roll Hall of Fame

Reaching Out

Writer John Rockwell, writing in the New York Times *in 1982, reflects on the Beatles' mixture of simplicity and sophistication. The article is reprinted in* The Lennon Companion.

"If any one thing can be said to define their compositional gift, it is the way they managed to adhere to basics yet to transcend crude simplicity by all manner of deft extensions and dislocations of the expected. . . .

In their cellar-dwelling Hamburg years, and even on their first couple of LPs with Ringo, The Beatles were a fierce little rock and roll band, one that could match the young Rolling Stones blues lick for blues lick. Later, as they expanded into a cultural phenomenon, their commitment to the narrow, strict directness of rock lessened, and for that they have been excoriated [condemned] by rock purists.

But it was that very diversification that ensured their universality. Their . . . willingness to reach out to a mass audience that craved pop ballads rather than the ruder passions of rock, allowed them to speak to almost everyone.

Reaching out to everybody may not be a central goal for an elitist, but The Beatles were the best and greatest of populists. They and their decade believed not simply that the finest art is the most popular art. . . . By reaching wide, The Beatles reached deep [and speak] to us as powerfully and privately today as they did two decades ago."

Crowds read the headlines outside Lennon's apartment after he was assassinated in 1980.

and again in 1995, when a lengthy TV documentary about the band aired amidst massive publicity. Along with the documentary came the first of three sets of double-CD compilations of rare and unreleased material. These featured two songs on which the surviving Beatles added backing to two John Lennon vocals recorded shortly before his death. Until then, the nearest the Beatles had come to a reunion was on 1973's *Ringo*, when Paul had played on one cut, George and John on another.

For the generations of musicians who have followed the Beatles, the band has always been a guiding light. There have been countless bands that have aspired to being Beatlesque, through their style or in popularity. Many have been gifted, and many have been popular. It is possible, though, that no band will ever reach the public's heart the way the Beatles once did, because the world has lost something since the relatively innocent days when the four lads from Liverpool ruled everything they saw.

The Beatles existed on three levels—as a social phenomenon, as individual personalities, and as musicians. The Beatles phenomenon has become nostalgic history, and their personalities no longer exist or have changed; their music, however, remains timeless.

Notes

Introduction: Meet the Beatles

1. Quoted in Mark Hertsgaard, *A Day in the Life*. New York: Delacorte, 1995, p. 146.

Chapter 1: Beginnings

2. Quoted in Geoffrey Stokes, *The Beatles*. New York: Rolling Stone Press/Times Books, 1980, p. 5.
3. Quoted in Hunter Davies, *The Beatles*. New York: McGraw-Hill, 1978, p. 13.
4. Quoted in Davies, *The Beatles*, p. 18.
5. Quoted in Davies, *The Beatles*, p. 30.
6. Quoted in Philip Norman, *Shout!* New York: Simon and Schuster, 1981, p. 34.
7. Quoted in Norman, *Shout!*, p. 44.
8. Quoted in Davies, *The Beatles*, p. 32.
9. Quoted in Norman, *Shout!*, p. 68.

Chapter 2: Hamburg and the Cavern Club

10. Quoted in Gareth L. Pawlowski, *How They Became the Beatles*. New York: Dutton, 1989, p. 25.
11. Norman, *Shout!*, p. 91.
12. Quoted in Pawlowski, *How They Became the Beatles*, p. 33.
13. Quoted in Pawlowski, *How They Became the Beatles*, p. 59.

Chapter 3: Becoming Famous

14. Brian Epstein, *A Cellarful of Noise*. Ann Arbor, MI: Pierian Press, 1984, p. 46.
15. Quoted in Norman, *Shout!*, p. 140.
16. Quoted in Pawlowski, *How They Became the Beatles*, p. 72.
17. George Martin, *All You Need Is Ears*. New York: St. Martin's Press, 1979, p. 122.
18. Quoted in Davies, *The Beatles*, p. 151.

19. Chet Flippo, *Yesterday*. New York: Doubleday, 1988, p. 172.

Chapter 4: Capturing England

20. Quoted in Martin, *All You Need Is Ears*, p. 126.
21. Martin, *All You Need Is Ears*, p. 127.
22. Martin, *All You Need Is Ears*, p. 130.
23. Quoted in Norman, *Shout!*, p. 191.
24. Quoted in Flippo, *Yesterday*, p. 175.
25. Quoted in Hertsgaard, *A Day in the Life*, p. 113.
26. Quoted in Pawlowski, *How They Became the Beatles*, p. 136.
27. Quoted in Pawlowski, *How They Became the Beatles*, p. 132.
28. Quoted in Norman, *Shout!*, p. 185.
29. Quoted in Pawlowski, *How They Became the Beatles*, p. 156.
30. Quoted in Davies, *The Beatles*, p. 200.
31. Quoted in Pawlowski, *How They Became the Beatles*, p. 150.
32. Quoted in Norman, *Shout!*, p. 106.

Chapter 5: Invading America

33. Quoted in Martin, *All You Need Is Ears*, p. 159.
34. Quoted in Norman, *Shout!*, p. 214.
35. Quoted in Flippo, *Yesterday*, p. 182.
36. Quoted in Norman, *Shout!*, p. 221.
37. Quoted in Hertsgaard, *A Day in the Life*, p. 91.
38. Quoted in Norman, *Shout!*, p. 224.

Chapter 6: The Beatlemania Years

39. Peter Brown with Steven Gaines, *The Love You Make*. New York: McGraw-Hill, 1983, p. 138.
40. Quoted in Norman, *Shout!*, p. 246.

41. Brown, *The Love You Make*, p. 140.

42. Quoted in Norman, *Shout!*, p. 239.

43. Quoted in Epstein, *A Cellarful of Noise*, p. 100.

Chapter 7: Controversy and Change

44. Quoted in *Playboy, Playboy Interviews.* Chicago: Playboy Press, 1967, p. 388.

45. Stokes, *The Beatles*, p. 151.

46. Quoted in Norman, *Shout!*, p. 265.

47. Quoted in Nicholas Schaffner, *The Beatles Forever.* Harrisburg, PA: Stackpole Books, 1977, p. 57.

48. Quoted in Geoffrey Guiliano, ed., *The Lost Beatles Interviews.* New York: Dutton, 1994, p. 72.

49. Quoted in Brown, *The Love You Make*, pp. 212–13.

50. Quoted in Flippo, *Yesterday*, p. 285.

51. Davies, *The Beatles*, p. 215.

Chapter 8: The Summer of Love and Death

52. Epstein, *A Cellarful of Noise*, p. 121.

53. George Martin, *With a Little Help from My Friends.* Boston: Little, Brown, 1994, p. 27.

54. Quoted in Norman, *Shout!*, p. 290.

55. Quoted in Martin, *With a Little Help from My Friends*, p. 168.

56. Quoted in Martin, *With a Little Help from My Friends*, p. 100.

57. Quoted in Martin, *With a Little Help from My Friends*, p. 110.

58. Quoted in Norman, *Shout!*, pp. 292–93.

59. Quoted in Jann Wenner, *Lennon Remembers.* San Francisco: Straight Arrow Books, 1971, p. 51.

Chapter 9: Drifting Apart

60. Quoted in Norman, *Shout!*, pp. 316–17.

61. Quoted in Wenner, *Lennon Remembers*, p. 56.

62. Quoted in Norman, *Shout!*, p. 324.

63. Quoted in Brown, *The Love You Make*, p. 240.

64. Quoted in Norman, *Shout!*, p. 347.

65. Quoted in Schaffner, *The Beatles Forever*, p. 118.

66. Quoted in Stokes, *The Beatles*, p. 215.

Chapter 10: The Breakup

67. Quoted in Norman, *Shout!*, p. 359.

68. Quoted in Norman, *Shout!*, p. 366.

69. Quoted in Norman, *Shout!*, p. 366.

70. Quoted in Brown, *The Love You Make*, p. 374.

71. Quoted in Norman, *Shout!*, p. 385.

72. Quoted in Hertsgaard, *A Day in the Life*, p. 244.

73. Quoted in Hertsgaard, *A Day in the Life*, p. 279.

74. Quoted in Norman, *Shout!*, p. 390.

75. Quoted in Schaffner, *The Beatles Forever*, p. 138.

76. Quoted in Norman, *Shout!*, p. 393.

Epilogue: After the Beatles

77. Quoted in Hertsgaard, *A Day in the Life*, p. 140.

78. Quoted in Brown, *The Love You Make*, p. 381.

For Further Reading

Ted Greenwald, *The Beatles Companion.* New York: Smithmark Books, 1992. A large, heavily illustrated book of trivia.

Dezo Hoffman, *With the Beatles.* New York: Omnibus, 1982. An anthology of historic photos with brief texts by a photographer who accompanied the Beatles extensively during the early part of their career.

John Lennon, *The Writings of John Lennon.* New York: Simon & Schuster, 1981. A compilation of Lennon's two books of poetry, stories, and drawings—*In His Own Write* and *A Spaniard in the Works.* This edition, published shortly after Lennon's death, has an introduction by Paul McCartney.

Nancy Loewen, *The Beatles.* Vero Beach, FL: Rourke Enterprises, 1989. For young adults.

Nicholas Schaffner, *The Beatles Forever.* Harrisburg, PA: Stackpole Books, 1977. A scrapbook-style collection of memorabilia and anecdotes that focuses on the impact the Beatles made on pop culture.

———, *The Boys from Liverpool: John, Paul, George, Ringo.* New York: Methuen, 1980. For young adults.

Geoffrey Stokes, *The Beatles.* New York: Rolling Stone Press/Times Books, 1980. A large and lavishly illustrated critical biography by a veteran *Rolling Stone* writer.

John Tobler, *The Beatles.* New York: Simon & Schuster, 1984. A large illustrated history by a British rock journalist.

Works Consulted

Peter Brown with Steven Gaines, *The Love You Make*. New York: McGraw-Hill, 1983. A bizarrely structured memoir by the longtime director of the Beatles' management company.

Ray Coleman, *Lennon*. New York: Harper-Perennial, 1992. An excellent biography of John Lennon by a British journalist.

Hunter Davies, *The Beatles*. New York: McGraw-Hill, 1978. A revised edition of the authorized biography. Heavily censored but basically factual. Originally written in 1968, with a short chapter added to bring its history up to 1978.

Brian Epstein, *A Cellarful of Noise*. Ann Arbor, MI: Pierian Press, 1984. A memoir, ghostwritten by Beatles press officer Derek Taylor and first published in 1964, by the Beatles' longtime manager.

Chet Flippo, *Yesterday*. New York: Doubleday, 1988. An unauthorized biography of Paul McCartney by a veteran rock writer.

Geoffrey Guiliano, ed., *The Lost Beatles Interviews*. New York: Dutton, 1994. A misleadingly titled book, padded with kiss-and-tell junk but with a few good sections.

George Harrison, *I, Me, Mine*. New York: Simon & Schuster, 1980. An autobiography by the only Beatle to write extensively about himself. Very odd, with Harrison's remembrances alternating with portions written by ex-Apple press agent Derek Taylor, and with a tone that varies from sweetness to bitterness.

Mark Hertsgaard, *A Day in the Life*. New York: Delacorte, 1995. A very well written, easily readable, extensively researched book that focuses on the music recorded by the Beatles.

Cynthia Lennon, *A Twist of Lennon*. New York: Avon, 1980. Paperback reprint of a heavily self-censored memoir published in 1978 by John Lennon's first wife.

George Martin, *All You Need Is Ears*. New York: St. Martin's Press, 1979. A memoir by the Beatles' longtime producer.

———, *With a Little Help from My Friends*. Boston: Little, Brown, 1994. A detailed look at the making of the groundbreaking *Sgt. Pepper* album.

Charles P. Neises, ed., *The Beatles Reader*. Ann Arbor, MI: Pierian Press, 1984. A collection from early years to mid-eighties of essays, news, and reviews. Poorly organized and too heavily reliant on American material but useful.

Philip Norman, *Shout!* New York: Simon and Schuster, 1981. Easily the most thorough, fully researched, and fair-minded of all the books on the Beatles.

Gareth L. Pawlowski, *How They Became the Beatles*. New York: Dutton, 1989. An obsessively detailed history of the Beatles' early years. Worth looking at for the wonderful early memorabilia, including newspaper clippings, photos, and posters.

Playboy, Playboy Interviews. Chicago: Playboy Press, 1967. Includes a 1965 interview with the Beatles, conducted by the American humor writer Jean Shepherd.

Tim Riley, *Tell Me Why*. New York: Knopf, 1988. Concentrates on the recorded output of the Beatles.

Ron Schaumberg, *Growing Up with the Beatles*. New York: Perigee/Putnam, 1976. An anecdotal history of the pop culture of Beatlemania.

Tom Schultheiss, *The Beatles: A Day in the Life*. New York: Quick Fox, 1981. A day-by-day diary of the Beatles' every move from 1960 to 1970, compiled by a noted Beatles expert.

Neville Stannard, *The Long and Winding Road*. London: Virgin Books, 1982. A dull but thoroughly detailed account of the Beatles' work on record, including bootlegs.

Elizabeth Thomson and David Gutman, eds., *The Lennon Companion*. New York: Macmillan, 1987. A collection of writings about Lennon. Heavily reliant on British sources that regard Lennon with a strong political slant.

Jann Wenner, *Lennon Remembers*. San Francisco: Straight Arrow Books, 1971. A compilation of two interviews in late 1970 and early 1971 from *Rolling Stone* conducted by the magazine's founder and editor.

Index

Picture Credits

Cover photo: Archive Photos

AP/Wide World Photos, 41, 49, 67, 68, 70, 114

Archive Photos, 10, 20, 24, 29, 31, 39, 45, 47, 62, 75, 103, 108, 110

Archive Photos/Express Newspapers, 15, 58, 65, 85, 96, 101, 102, 104

Archive Photos/Fotos International, 113

Archive Photos/Frank Driggs, 93

Archive Photos/Popperfoto, 23, 33, 36, 53, 71, 83

Corbis-Bettmann, 19

Penguin/Corbis-Bettmann, 38

Photofest, 14, 30, 57, 89, 91, 97, 115

UPI/Corbis-Bettmann, 48, 54, 55, 77, 78, 80, 82, 95, 99, 117

About the Author

Adam Woog lives in Seattle, Washington, with his wife and daughter. He remembers precisely the first time he heard a Beatles record. The first single and the first album he ever bought were both by the Beatles.

Woog is the author of over a dozen books for young people and adults. For Lucent Books, he has written *The United Nations*, *Poltergeists*, *The Importance of Harry Houdini*, *The Importance of Louis Armstrong*, *The Importance of Duke Ellington*, *The Importance of Elvis Presley*, *The Mysterious Death of Amelia Earhart*, and *The Mysterious Death of Marilyn Monroe*.